FLANNERY O'CONNOR

FLANNERY O'CONNOR

A Biography

Melissa Simpson

GREENWOOD BIOGRAPHIES

GREENWOOD PRESS
WESTPORT, CONNECTICUT · LONDON

Library of Congress Cataloging-in-Publication Data

Simpson, Melissa.
   Flannery O'Connor : a biography / Melissa Simpson.
     p. cm. — (Greenwood biographies, ISSN 1540–4900)
   Includes bibliographical references (p.) and index.
   ISBN 0–313–32999–0 (alk. paper)
   1. O'Connor, Flannery. 2. Authors, American—20th century—Biography.
   3. Milledgeville (Ga.)—Biography. I. Title. II. Series.
   PS3565.C57Z863   2005
   813'.54—dc22   2005016820

British Library Cataloguing in Publication Data is available.

Library of Congress Catalog Card Number: 2005016820
ISBN: 0–313–32999–0
ISSN: 1540–4900

05-06

First published in 2005

Greenwood Press, 88 Post Road West, Westport, CT 06881
An imprint of Greenwood Publishing Group, Inc.
www.greenwood.com

Printed in the United States of America

The paper used in this book complies with the
Permanent Paper Standard issued by the National
Information Standards Organization (Z39.48–1984).

10   9   8   7   6   5   4   3   2   1

For Kevin, Hannah, and Wade, my beloved ones

CONTENTS

Photo essay follows page 79

SERIES FOREWORD

In response to high school and public library needs, Greenwood developed this distinguished series of full-length biographies specifically for student use. Prepared by field experts and professionals, these engaging biographies are tailored for high school students who need challenging yet accessible biographies. Ideal for secondary school assignments, the length, format, and subject areas are designed to meet educators' requirements and students' interests.

Greenwood offers an extensive selection of biographies spanning all curriculum related subject areas including social studies, the sciences, literature and the arts, history and politics, as well as popular culture, covering public figures and famous personalities from all time periods and backgrounds, both historic and contemporary, who have made an impact on American and/or world culture. Greenwood biographies were chosen based on comprehensive feedback from librarians and educators. Consideration was given to both curriculum relevance and inherent interest. The result is an intriguing mix of the well known and the unexpected, the saints and sinners from long-ago history and contemporary pop culture. Readers will find a wide array of subject choices from fascinating crime figures like Al Capone to inspiring pioneers like Margaret Mead, from the greatest minds of our time like Stephen Hawking to the most amazing success stories of our day like J.K. Rowling.

While the emphasis is on fact, not glorification, the books are meant to be fun to read. Each volume provides in-depth information about the subject's life from birth through childhood, the teen years, and adulthood.

A thorough account relates family background and education, traces personal and professional influences, and explores struggles, accomplishments, and contributions. A timeline highlights the most significant life events against a historical perspective. Bibliographies supplement the reference value of each volume.

PREFACE

In April 1964, Flannery O'Connor penned a letter to her close friend Maryat Lee from her sickbed, saying that her family was full of people who "creak along" to be around 96 years old.[1] Little did she know that she would not live to be 96 but would be dead in a scarce four months at age 39. The lupus she had suffered with for 14 years had been reactivated by a necessary surgery, causing her to be admitted to the hospital on and off throughout 1964 and to die on August 3rd of that year.

At her death, America lost one of its most controversial, most misunderstood, and most promising young writers. Though she was largely confined to Andalusia, the Milledgeville, Georgia, farm she shared with her mother, O'Connor entertained visitors, lectured at colleges and universities around the country, cultivated numerous friendships, and published two novels, a collection of short stories, and other miscellaneous prose before her death. While such a small body of publications hardly seems much of an accomplishment, she carved an indelible niche for herself in American literature. Rarely concerning herself with critical or public reception of her work, O'Connor carried out what she felt was her mission in life: to share her faith with a world that had strayed from the basic beliefs of Christianity. Ironically, her message was misunderstood by many, chiefly Catholics, who were offended by her use of shocking, grotesque Southern characters, her use of violent situations, and her acerbic wit. In addition, efforts to classify O'Connor as part of a "movement," such as the Southern Agrarian movement or the Southern Gothic School, have all ultimately failed. While her work may contain elements of different literary movements, her work has broken free of any box in which people have tried to confine it. O'Connor was a Southern writer for certain but felt that her message far transcended time and place, and she strove always to remain true to the beliefs she held dear. As O'Connor's childhood friend Betty Boyd Love has said, "Flannery was never on the fence about people or issues or social patterns or institutions. She gave those she could believe an abiding loyalty; she gave those she couldn't credit the back of her verbal hand."[2] Despite her physical limitations, O'Connor devoted herself to her life's work, deliberately making writing the top priority in her daily activities, second only to her faith, up until the time of her death.

The research materials for this examination of O'Connor's life are from four main sources: her letters collected in *The Habit of Being*; her occasional prose collected in *Mystery and Manners*; her short stories assembled in *The Collected Works*; and journal and magazine articles, many of which are available in the Flannery O'Connor Collection at Georgia College and State University in Milledgeville.

NOTES

1. Letter to Maryat Lee, April 16, 1964, in *The Habit of Being: Letters of Flannery O'Connor*, ed. Sally Fitzgerald (New York: Farrar, Straus, and Giroux, 1979), p. 151.

2. Betty Boyd Love, "Recollections of Flannery O'Connor," *Flannery O'Connor Bulletin* XIV (1985): 66.

ACKNOWLEDGMENTS

In many ways, any book is a collaborative effort, and it is a pleasure for me to have people to thank for partnering with me on this project in one way or another.

Many thanks go to my friends and colleagues Sheryl Murtha, Laura Shelton, and especially Michelle Cearley for their ideas concerning the direction this review of O'Connor's life should take; to my best friends Wynter Cavin, for her endless encouragement and willingness to share her chocolate and her writer's heart, and Shanon Key, for her wit and her ability to think differently than I do (and to tell me exactly what she's thinking); and to the friends who support me and fill my life with laughter and joy, no matter what the task at hand: Tanya Helms, Christy Melder, Randi Mackey, Deborah Fletcher, Cheri Mason, and Julie Milnes.

I also offer my gratitude to my mentors Diane Spriggs and Kathy Latimer; to my mother Jessie High for her interest in this project, travel companionship, and babysitting assistance; and to Tammy Wyatt and Nancy Davis Bray of Georgia College and State University for their help in utilizing the Flannery O'Connor Collection and in gathering photographs for this book. My supreme thanks goes to my husband, Kevin, and children, Hannah and Wade, for their enduring love, for always treasuring what I treasure, and for graciously sharing their time with me so that I could complete this project; and above all, I thank God for the gifts and blessings He so graciously gives that I do not deserve.

TIMELINE: EVENTS IN THE LIFE OF FLANNERY O'CONNOR

March 25, 1925	Born Mary Flannery O'Connor to Edward F. and Regina O'Connor in Savannah, Georgia
1931	Begins first grade at St. Vincent's Grammar School in Savannah
1936	Transfers to Sacred Heart School
1938	Moves to Atlanta and then to Milledgeville; enrolls in Peabody High School
1941	Edward O'Connor dies of lupus
1942	Graduates from Peabody High School and enters Georgia State College for Women in Milledgeville
1945	Graduates from Georgia State College for Women with an A.B.
1945–48	Attends Writer's Workshop at State University of Iowa
1946	First story, "The Geranium," is published in *Accent*
1947	Earns M.F.A. from State University of Iowa
	Wins $750 Rinehart-Iowa Fiction Award for what would become *Wise Blood*
1948	Goes to the Yaddo Artists' Colony in Saratoga Springs, New York, in June
1949	Chapters of *Wise Blood* are published in *Partisan Review*; leaves Yaddo in February and moves to New York City and then to Ridgefield, Connecticut, to live with Sally and Robert Fitzgerald; is operated on for a floating kidney

1950	Experiences first attack of lupus in December
1951	Returns to Milledgeville and is officially diagnosed with lupus
1952	*Wise Blood* is published; orders her first peafowl
1953	Is awarded $2,000 Kenyon Fellowship
1954	"A Circle in the Fire" is awarded second prize in the O'Henry awards for short stories
1955	*A Good Man is Hard to Find* is published; begins walking with crutches
1957	Receives $1,000 National Institute for Arts and Letters grant; "Greenleaf" wins first prize in the O'Henry awards
1958	Travels with her mother to Lourdes, Rome, and other major European cities; has an audience with the Pope; passes driving test on second try
1959	Receives $8,000 Ford Foundation grant
1960	*The Violent Bear It Away* is published
1963	"Everything that Rises Must Converge" wins first prize in the O'Henry awards
August 3, 1964	Dies in Milledgeville, Georgia, hospital after lupus is reactivated following an operation several weeks earlier to remove a fibroid ovarian tumor
1965	*Everything that Rises Must Converge* is published; "Revelation" wins first prize in the O'Henry awards
1969	*Mystery and Manners: The Occasional Prose of Flannery O'Connor* is published
1971	*The Complete Stories of Flannery O'Connor* is published, wins National Book Award
1979	*The Habit of Being: Letters of Flannery O'Connor* is published
1983	*The Presence of Grace and Other Book Reviews by Flannery O'Connor* is published

Sources: Modern Critical Views: Flannery O'Connor, ed. Harold Bloom (New York: Chelsea House, 1986), pp. 145–46; *Conversations with Flannery O'Connor*, ed. Rosemary M. Magee (Jackson: University Press of Mississippi, 1987), pp. xxv–xxvii; "Chronology," *Collected Works*, ed. Sally Fitzgerald (New York: Library of America, 1988), pp. 1237–56.

Chapter 1

EARLY LIFE

While we tend to think of Flannery O'Connor as marked by distinction because of her work, her life was marked by distinction from the moment she was born on March 25, 1925, to Edward F. and Regina Cline O'Connor in Savannah, Georgia. O'Connor was born into a long line of distinguished Irish Catholics who began immigrating to Georgia in the 1700s, approximately 200 years before her birth. Catholics were officially excluded from the colony by law, along with Blacks, rum, and attorneys. According to O'Connor scholar Sally Fitzgerald, these groups were feared and were not trusted after the Reformation, hence the creation of such laws.[1] In addition, Britain's primary nemesis at the time resided in Georgia's neighboring state of Florida: Spanish Catholics who had converted many Native Americans to Catholicism. Colonial officials may have even feared that Georgia Catholics might unite with the Spanish and even the nearby French Catholics and thereby jeopardize the well-being of the colony. Despite regulations against their presence, Catholics made their way into Georgia anyway, making sure not to draw attention to their religious affiliation yet creating an image of themselves as mischievous, perhaps because many among their number were Irish convicts. In 1752, the colony was restored to the British crown, and for whatever reason, regulations against Catholics were relaxed. Catholics were even encouraged to come to Savannah after carnage took place in Santo Domingo.[2] These influxes paved the way for the establishment of a strong Catholic presence in what would later become the heart of America's Bible belt.

ANCESTRY

Flannery O'Connor's ancestors were part of this original group of Catholics, and she was always pleased that "the families who came together in her person participated so fully in the post-Colonial social, religious, educational, commercial, and military history of the state itself."[3] O'Connor's maternal great-grandfather, Peter Cline, came to Georgia in 1845 to teach Latin. He died in 1848, and among his surviving children was Peter James Cline, Regina O'Connor's father, who opened a dry goods store in Milledgeville in 1891. He became a prominent citizen and was elected mayor of the city in 1888. He first married Kate Treanor and, after her death, married her younger sister Margaret Ida, who was the mother of Regina O'Connor. Combined, the two women bore him 16 children.

On the other side of Flannery O'Connor's prominent family, we find John Flannery, who came to America with his father in 1851 to escape famine conditions in Ireland. Flannery fought for the Confederacy in the Civil War and eventually became captain of the 1st Volunteer Regiment of Georgia. After the war, he founded Southern Bank of the State of Georgia and joined the cotton trade as founder and president of the John Flannery Company. While those business accomplishments are certainly impressive, his successes do not end there. He was very active in community and civic activities, such as the Georgia Historical Society and the Irish-American Historical Society, and was a director of several railroad companies. Perhaps most important was his involvement in the local Catholic church. The Cathedral of St. John the Baptist was built in Savannah in the mid-1870s and was largely funded by Flannery. The church burned in 1898, and Flannery was instrumental in seeing that it was rebuilt. In the mean time, he married Mary Ellen Norton in 1867, and it was for her that Mary Flannery O'Connor was named.

During this time, more of O'Connor's ancestors were stirring in the annals of the state of Georgia. Her paternal great-grandfather, Patrick O'Connor, came to Savannah from Ireland in the mid 1800s, and he and his brother Daniel bought a great deal of property and ran a successful business. His son Edward Francis, Flannery O'Connor's paternal grandfather, was a well-known businessman in Savannah, where he was president of the People's Bank and later director of the Hibernia Bank. At the wedding of his daughter Nan to Herbert Cline of Milledgeville, his son Edward Francis, Jr., met Regina Cline. Of course, the two married in 1922 and became the parents of Mary Flannery O'Connor.

PARENTS

Relatively little is known about O'Connor's father. He attended Catholic schools in Savannah and went to college at St. Mary's in Maryland. According to Sally Fitzgerald, photographs reveal him as a good-looking man "with the same direct gaze that his daughter inherited."[4] He was part of the American Expeditionary Force in World War I and, after the war, became strongly involved in the American Legion, in addition to the real estate business through which he supported his wife and daughter. As a highly involved member of the American Legion and eventually Commander of the American Legion for the state of Georgia, Edward O'Connor was involved in numerous community activities and spoke to groups throughout Georgia; surviving copies of his speeches show that he possessed a lucid, keen mind and writing style.[5] Katherine Doyle Groves, a cousin of O'Connor's, remembers him as detached and a bit haughty, despite the fact that he always seemed involved in some sort of failed business endeavor. Others recall him as hardworking, though he always took an afternoon nap, which may have been early evidence of the lupus with which he was diagnosed in 1938 and from which he died in 1941 at age 45.[6] He seemed to dote on his only child, giving her her own listing in the Savannah City Directory (equivalent to a modern day telephone directory) and carrying her drawings and poems around with him, many of which she put under his napkin at the dinner table. For some reason, the adult O'Connor rarely discussed her father, but she did write to her friend Betty Hester in 1956 that her writing accomplishments pleased her more than they might have ordinarily, because she felt she was fulfilling some of the goals her father never accomplished. Although he died when she was only 15, O'Connor seemed to feel a bond with him still, especially after she was diagnosed with lupus.

O'Connor scholar and biographer Jean Cash maintains that while O'Connor and her father were close, the women wielded the real power in the family. According to Cash, Regina and Edward O'Connor chose to name their daughter Mary Flannery, after cousin Kate Semmes's mother, to win over Semmes so that she would offer them steady financial assistance. While Semmes did have a great deal of influence in the life of the O'Connors, both financial and otherwise, it was Regina who influenced her daughter the most. Friends and family members recall her as very controlling of O'Connor as a child, keeping a close eye on O'Connor's friends, making her eat all of her vegetables before eating anything else, taking her to school every day even though it was in walking distance, and not allowing her to have pets because of potential germs, for example. While Regina's controlling nature was a source of conflict when O'Connor was an adult, she seems not to have minded it as a child, at least according to friends and family who remember the mother-daughter relationship as close and "mutually dependant."[7]

EARLY SCHOOLING

Little is known about O'Connor's infancy, but more information is available about her life after 1931 when she began school in Savannah at St. Vincent's Grammar School which was operated by the Mercy Order of Nuns. Schoolmates of O'Connor's have various, often contradictory memories of her as an elementary school student. For example, Lillian Dowling Odom remembers O'Connor not playing well with others and purposefully isolating herself so she could spend time reading, while Loretta Feuger Hoynes remembers her getting along with other children and leading a normal existence, other than going to her nearby home for lunch, unlike the other children who ate lunch at school. Perhaps intimating her sense of humor as an adult, O'Connor was a mischievous student, chewing snuff in class, bringing her teachers tomatoes instead of apples, and shooting rubber bands from her braces behind the nuns' backs. It appears that her impish behavior did remain behind the nuns' backs, at least for the most part, for Sister Consolata, one of O'Connor's teachers at St. Vincent's, remembers her as being a fairly normal, well-behaved student who did, however, have an uncommon interest in chickens. Not surprisingly, Sister Consolata remembers O'Connor as especially adept at reading and writing and as "speaking to adults as though she was on the same level with them."[8]

After completing fifth grade, O'Connor transferred to Sacred Heart Grammar School for Girls; the reasons given for her transfer vary depending on whom one asks. For example, some suggest that she transferred because her closest friends did; others say she transferred because Sacred Heart was a more prestigious school than St. Vincent's and had better teachers; still others say that the strictness of the nuns at St. Vincent's prompted the move. Regardless of the reasons, O'Connor did transfer and was transported to school every day in Kate Semmes's electric car, which was certainly an anomaly since everyone else with a car had one powered by gasoline.

While O'Connor did have friendships in her school days in Savannah, few of them seem to have been close, and several appear to have been forced by her mother. One example was Newell Turner Parr, a non-Catholic girl who lived across the street from the O'Connors. Even though Regina approved of the friendship, Parr felt that she and O'Connor had little in common. For example, O'Connor wanted Parr to sit in her bedroom as O'Connor read her stories that she had written, but Parr was simply not interested. Another friend, Elizabeth Maguire Johnson, also lived near the O'Connors and visited their home often to play with young Flannery. Johnson recalls a much meaner O'Connor than her other friends: in one visit, Johnson brought along another friend, whom O'Connor promptly tied to a chair in her bedroom. Yet another friend, previously mentioned Loretta Feuger Hoynes, was forced to play with O'Connor in Savannah and was even forced by her mother to visit O'Connor every summer after the O'Connors moved to Milledgeville. Readers of O'Connor's story "A Temple of the Holy Ghost" will recognize one memorable instance in which a teenage Hoynes went to the movies with the brother of a friend of the O'Connors. After the movie, the pair wanted to sit in the front porch swing and smoke, prompting O'Connor to put Hoynes' suitcase on the front porch, declare her a "wayward woman," and for all intents and purposes, kick Hoynes out of her house.[9]

Hoynes describes the young O'Connor as profound, eccentric, stubborn, and even a bit unapproachable, yet others describe her as imaginative, authentic, humorous, and down-to-earth. These seeming contradictions point to a truth that would be borne out as O'Connor aged: she was a multifaceted, complex person who could indeed be *all* of these things, who cared little for acting like anyone other than who she was, and who had a knack for discerning the true nature of people and situations. Without a doubt, family and friends recognized the genius and talent she possessed, even as a child, though few expected it to bring her the celebrity that it did.

ON THE MOVE

At this point in O'Connor's life, her family moved several times. In 1938, her father began working for the Federal Housing Administration as a real estate appraiser, precipitating a move for the family from Savannah to Atlanta. O'Connor attended St. Joseph's Church school in Atlanta during the seventh grade, but she and her mother moved to Milledgeville, Georgia's Confederate capital, once the school year ended to join the matriarchal household of Regina's two unmarried sisters, Mary and Katie Cline, in the family's house on Greene Street, a white mansion which is now officially known as the Gordon-Ward-Beal-Cline-O'Connor House. Edward O'Connor stayed in Atlanta during the week and joined

O'Connor and Regina in Milledgeville on weekends. According to Cash, Milledgeville residents remember little of Edward O'Connor, mostly because he was there so seldom. There is also no record of how well the young O'Connor adapted to these changes in residence.

Because there were no parochial schools in Milledgeville, O'Connor enrolled in Peabody High School in 1938. Peabody was 1 of 10 "experimental schools" in Georgia and had close ties to Georgia State College for Women (GSCW), also in Milledgeville. Because most boys in town attended Georgia Military Academy, Peabody's student body was primarily composed of girls. Most teachers had advanced degrees and appear to have been much more educated than most Georgia teachers at the time. In addition, a GSCW professor supervised a set of six teachers, all of whom rotated from class to class, giving students a new instructor in each subject about every six weeks. With the school's flexible curriculum, students often chose what they were taught based on what they wanted to learn about instead of being taught material mandated by the state. While many former students look back on their educations at Peabody with fondness, O'Connor consistently lamented the lack of guidance she received and criticized its "progressive" nature, especially its neglect of the classics and history, which she saw as indispensable in a writer's education. While O'Connor's sentiments were perhaps an exaggeration, she nevertheless remained consistently dissatisfied with her Peabody education throughout her life.

AN ARTIST EMERGES

Despite her lingering reservations about the educational philosophies being put into practice at Peabody, the permissive atmosphere did allow O'Connor to develop her early skills as a visual artist. As the art editor of the *Peabody Palladium*, she was able to include several of her cartoons, a medium she would continue to refine, and in addition, several issues included her essays and reviews. These publications seem appropriate since this is where O'Connor's interests were as a teenager: writing and cartooning. While "proper" girls were partial to piano or dancing lessons and boys, O'Connor was not. In fact, it was only after Regina forced her into piano and dancing lessons that she begrudgingly complied, and she displayed little interest in the opposite sex. In fact, Cash claims that O'Connor's having the heroine kiss a chicken in one of the stories she wrote as a teenager indicates her "deliberate rejection of sexuality."[10] Her lack of interest in boys has been interpreted as the result of her father's death, as the result of her living in a household of women, and as latent homosexuality. It may be impossible to determine for sure the source of her lack of interest, but one thing remains certain: even as a child, O'Connor simply focused on what was interesting to *her*, whether anyone else approved or not.

When O'Connor became interested in something, the time she would give to it could be called nothing less than wholehearted devotion. Of course, a vast amount of attention has been given to her dedication to her writing; much less has been given to the fascination with cartooning that she displayed in her youth. As many children do, she drew a great deal as a small child, but while many children outgrow such interests, O'Connor's interests in the visual arts seemed to only increase as she aged. Apparently, there were artists in her family, but their work must not have appealed to O'Connor since she was careful to paint over any cracks in the walls at home in an attempt to keep her mother from covering the cracks with relatives' artwork.[11] As previously mentioned, she was art editor of the *Peabody Palladium,* where she produced her cartoons using a technique called linoleum cutting or linocut. In this process, an image is cut into a piece of linoleum, which is easier to cut than wood. Ink is rolled over the raised parts that remain on the surface of the linoleum after it is cut. These parts are printed, and the image is then transferred to paper when the paper is pressed on to the area covered in ink.

GEORGIA STATE COLLEGE FOR WOMEN

After graduating from Peabody, O'Connor entered an accelerated program at Georgia State College for Women in the summer of 1942, even though it is likely that she considered other schools. However, the travel problems brought on by World War II, the expense of going to school elsewhere, the fact that O'Connor was only 16 at the time, and simple social convention probably all contributed to her enrollment in the local school, which is mere blocks from the Cline House. GSCW was a traditional college devoted primarily to training teachers, and like most schools in the 1940s, it took the place of parents by strictly supervising its students. For example, there were regulations on when men could visit the campus, when cars could be driven on campus, when students could go home for the weekend, what students could wear, and when students *had* to study each night.

While keeping up with her studies, primarily in English, social sciences, and education, O'Connor also continued to develop her skills as a visual artist. O'Connor painted some as an adult, and early evidence of this interest exists in her painting while a GSCW student. She was one of only three students to have a painting travel throughout Georgia as part of an exhibit,[12] and an alumnae journal from 1948 includes a picture of a mural painted by O'Connor in the student union; unfortunately, the mural was painted over before O'Connor became famous, and the student union building was demolished in the 1970s.

She did, however, find a more enduring medium in the school's newspaper, *The Colonnade*. Her cartoons, which she did with a more conventional charcoal or ink and paper technique, instead of linocut, appeared in nearly every issue while she was a student, beginning in October 1942, and were popular with students. They also frequently satirized the Women Accepted for Voluntary Service (WAVES),[13] who were stationed at GSCW when the U.S. Navy designated the campus as a site for clerical training, for their nonconformity and their disruption of the male-female ratios in Milledgeville. O'Connor was also often critical of students and faculty for their apathy and of the educational establishment in general for its promulgation of weak-mindedness. O'Connor did not reserve her critical eye for everyone but herself, however. In several of her cartoons, she pokes fun at herself, as in the one which portrays a social situation in which everyone is dancing except for a "bespectacled wallflower who grins behind her hand and asserts that she can always pursue a Ph.D."[14]

Aspects of O'Connor's personality and interests that find their way into her later writings are also evident in her early visual work. For example, her signature on the *Colonnade* cartoons consists of her initials, MFOC, formed into the shape of a bird, a childhood interest that she kept throughout her life. Like her fiction, her cartoons demonstrate her ability to illuminate the absurdities of social convention or of simple everyday life with a combination of seriousness and humor. While many of the instructors and administrators at GSCW appear to have looked at her cartooning with some disdain, O'Connor held a different opinion of the artistic medium. Even though she came from the area's "aristocracy," she despised pretentiousness and saw cartooning as just as valid as writing, charcoal sketching, or oil painting. O'Connor also drew illustrations for the Student Government Association, the YWCA, the Recreation Association, and the college yearbook, *The Spectrum*, during her senior year when she was features editor. Although several of her contemporaries expected her to find fame through her visual art, that focus eventually shifted to a near total focus on her written art; however, Robert Fitzgerald has noted that she admired the work of *New Yorker* cartoonist George Price a great deal, and of all the books in her personal library, only one is about art: a book on French artist Honore Daumier whose work helped shape the work of many cartoonists.[15]

While O'Connor was clearly involved in student activities and in tune with life on the GSCW campus, she remained detached from the social scene, living with her mother and aunts instead of in campus dormitories. She seems to have had no romantic attachments, but she did have several good friends, including Betty Boyd Love, who entered the accelerated program with her and became a regular visitor to her home along with several other students. According to Love, she and O'Connor wrote "dreadful" poetry and worked on the school's literary magazine together. While O'Connor's attachments may have been few, they seemed to run deep, as she and Love kept in touch throughout O'Connor's life. While many students of O'Connor's age surely wanted to blend in with their peers, O'Connor was nothing if not an individual. For example, GSCW tradition prescribed that all freshmen wear an onion around their necks and bow to sophomores on "Rat Day"; legend has it that O'Connor replied to the request, "I will not."[16] Love perhaps described her best:

> Completely aside from her formidable talent, Flannery O'Connor was a genuinely unusual individual, and I was fond of her. She knew who she was, and what she was, and was neither over-pleased nor disturbed by either.... There are critics who would have you believe she was a misfit, a bit of a freak herself. Not so! Physically, she was always a bit awkward. But she radiated a glow of good humor, compassion, and intelligence that made her very attractive.[17]

Academically, O'Connor did well at GSCW, earning an A.B. with a major in social sciences in 1945. She completed the degree in only three years because of the accelerated program, earned a spot on the dean's list every quarter but one, and was selected for the Phoenix Society, a GSCW honor society reserved for the top seven percent of graduating seniors. Several of her GSCW contemporaries have commented that she seemed more on the level of the faculty than the students, and she maintained a lifelong relationship with several of her professors, including Katherine Scott, who taught O'Connor's English 101 course. Like many of her instructors, Scott recognized O'Connor's genius but viewed her as somewhat "warped," an attitude that some believe stemmed from Scott's jealousy of O'Connor's success and disapproval of her writing style. On the other hand, instructors such as Hallie Smith, who taught creative writing, appeared to appreciate O'Connor's wit and irreverence and encouraged her to submit her work to the school's literary magazine, *The Corinthian*, which she did.

ON TO IOWA

One of O'Connor's professors did not have an especially close relationship with her but did have a marked impact on her future. Philosophy professor George Beiswanger earned his M.A. and Ph.D. from the University of Iowa, and he informed O'Connor of fellowships available at the university. Armed with a letter of recommendation from Beiswanger, O'Connor applied for a fellowship and received one, setting in motion a new era in her life as a writer. O'Connor began her studies in Iowa City in September 1945, entering one of the country's first programs devoted to creative writing, first called the Writer's Workshop in 1939. Paul Engle, who went through the program himself, was the director during O'Connor's years in Iowa and was passionate about getting the best students and the best lecturers for the program. O'Connor originally enrolled at the university in the journalism department but approached Engle rather soon after her arrival in Iowa City about becoming part of the Writer's Workshop. Engle tells a well-known story of their first meeting:

> She walked into my office one day and spoke to me. I understood nothing, not one syllable. As far as I knew, she was saying, "Aaaraaaraaarah." My God, I thought to myself, this is a retarded young girl.
> [...] Finally, I said, excuse me, my name is Paul Engle. I gave her a pad—believe me, this is true—and said would you please write down what you're telling me. And she wrote, "My name is Flannery O'Connor. I'm from Milledgeville, Georgia. I'm a writer." She didn't say "I want to be a writer." She said, "I am a writer."[18]

Despite the awkwardness of their first meeting, O'Connor was admitted to the program immediately, and her talent and genius soon became obvious, especially after she published her first short story, "The Geranium," in the magazine *Accent* during her first year at Iowa. Even though she was concentrating primarily on her writing now, she persisted in submitting cartoons to the art department and even took courses in American political cartooning and advanced drawing.[19] Most of her colleagues from the program remember her as a quiet student who often sat at the back of the room, the kind of person who made everyone else wonder what she was thinking because when she did speak, her comments were inordinately perceptive. She certainly stood out among the other students, many of whom were returning veterans of World War II who drank heavily and had absolutely no interest in the religious faith that was so dear to O'Connor. Andrew Lytle, a guest teacher in 1947, maintains that the

other students knew O'Connor's work was superior and, as a result, she
often intimidated them, especially the men.[20] O'Connor's friend Jean
Wylder comments that it was O'Connor's isolation from the other writers
that first attracted Wylder to her. Even as Wylder got to know O'Connor,
she seemed at times to exist on another plane, one higher than her fellow
students. As Wylder stated, "I would have liked to have gone to the
movies with her or had a Coke with her, but it simply didn't occur to
me that things like that could ever be a part of her life." Even her room
portrayed an almost monastic separateness: a tidily made bed and a desk
with a typewriter, the only luxury being the vanilla wafers she liked to
snack on as she wrote.[21]

Romantic relationships also did not seem to be part of O'Connor's life
while she was in Iowa, though she did develop several close friendships
while she was there, just as she did at GSCW. O'Connor lived several
places during her tenure at the University of Iowa: first in graduate student
housing and then in a boarding house. Her roommate in graduate student
housing, Martha Bell Spreiser, a business education student, did not have
a particularly close relationship with O'Connor because the two of them
were both engrossed in writing their theses. However, she does remember
O'Connor as funny, quiet, and devout. Perhaps most telling is that she
also recalls that distracting O'Connor from her work was a near impossible
feat. O'Connor's relationship with Jean Wylder developed during this
time as well, and even though Wylder considered herself O'Connor's
closest friend in Iowa, the two rarely socialized outside of the Workshop.
In fact, Wylder did not know until after O'Connor left Iowa that she was
a devout Catholic and attended mass every day.

O'Connor's romantic relationships were even more sparse than her
friendships. Just as the men in the Writer's Workshop were intimidated
by O'Connor, so were the men with whom friends tried to fix her up.
Particularly up for discussion is her relationship with Robie Macauley, with
whom O'Connor kept in contact throughout her life. Macauley once stated
in an interview that he "dated" O'Connor, yet he later told Jean Cash that
the two went to a few movies together and shared a few dinners but little
more. Walter Sullivan asserts that Macauley looked after O'Connor and
the two shared a very close, highly developed friendship because of their
similar interests and senses of humor. The two were close enough friends
that O'Connor read every chapter of *Wise Blood* to Macauley as they sat
on the porch of her boarding house. On the other hand, Sally Fitzgerald
believes that their relationship was more serious, at least from O'Connor's
point of view. This view seems questionable, however, since Macauley was
engaged in 1949, a fact of which O'Connor was well aware.[22]

O'Connor completed her M.F.A. in 1947, using a collection of six short stories entitled *The Geranium* as her thesis. Up until this point, O'Connor's work, which was fairly generic in its characters and settings, lacked the decidedly Southern essence so characteristic of her mature work. For example, her writings at GSCW, though mostly nonfiction, contain the biting satire readers have come to expect from O'Connor, but the fiction contains very flat, stereotypical black characters. Two stories in particular "have such thick artificial dialect that they totter painfully close to an Amos-and-Andy variety of racism." O'Connor's thesis contains a story set in the "backwoods," a story about a boy pursuing a turkey in a setting that is vague but *could* be construed as Southern, and an unmarried woman who wants to become a writer—nothing absolutely Southern in flavor. However, O'Connor scholar Virginia Wray contends that the eventual addition of "Southern" material to O'Connor's work resulted from the homesickness for her native Georgia that she experienced while in Iowa.[23]

After completing her M.F.A., O'Connor stayed in Iowa another year, thanks to a Rinehart-Iowa Fellowship in fiction that she received. Without a doubt, O'Connor's time in Iowa was pivotal to her career, if for nothing more than the people she met while she was there. For example, Paul Engle selected several of O'Connor's stories for the O. Henry collection while he was editor. In 1957–1958, 1962, and 1979, her stories were also included in the *Best American Short Stories* anthology. Engle often complained that O'Connor did not give the Workshop enough credit for launching her career, but it would have been unlike O'Connor to give overwhelming recognition to any single influence on her work, though she did acknowledge that her time in Iowa gave her the necessary confirmation that she could indeed be the writer she claimed to be.[24] In her essay "The Nature and Aim of Fiction," she registers her disapproval of writing classrooms in which students assess each other's work, much as they did in the Workshop, citing instead the importance of a teacher's negative influence on writers— "saying, 'This doesn't work because ...' or 'This does work because ...'" She claimed that student assessment of student work was often motivated by "ignorance, flattery, and spite."[25] In fact, her mixture of credit and criticism toward the Workshop illustrates the discernment she brought toward every institution of which she was a part and knew well.

YADDO

While O'Connor's time at Iowa jump-started her writing career, she was not content to stay there. In 1948, she requested admission to Yaddo, a Saratoga Springs, New York, artists colony. Spencer and Katrina Trask bought the 40-acre property in 1881 and conceived of converting it into a refuge for artists after their four children died. Although Spencer Trask died in 1909 and Katrina died in 1922, her second husband, George Foster Peabody, brought their dream to fruition and hired Elizabeth Ames as executive director, allowing Yaddo to host its first artists in 1926. The Yaddo Foundation pays for each artist's room and board, while the artists live on the property in cottages or in individual rooms in the 55-room main house so that they can wholeheartedly devote themselves to their work.[26] O'Connor lived at Yaddo during the summer of 1948 and lived there full-time from September 1948 to February 1949.

Even though O'Connor was able to personally fulfill the aim of the colony and dedicate herself to her work, she was uncomfortable with the behavior and beliefs of most people there. She detected pseudo-intellectualism, a quality she despised, in abundance, and most residents were liberal in their politics, if not outright supporters of Communism. In fact, in 1949, O'Connor was swept up in a scandal of sorts involving Communist activity at Yaddo. Largely aided by post-war anti-Communist sentiments, O'Connor found herself among a group that attempted to have Elizabeth Ames removed as director at Yaddo. With "egotistical messianic fervor," a somewhat mentally unstable Robert Lowell led the crusade, which was prompted by Ames's "special treatment" of Agnes Smedley, an outspoken Communist who frequently stayed at Yaddo from 1943 to 1948. Smedley had been accused in a recent *New York Times* article of organizing a group of Russian spies in Japan in 1942. Even though the *Times* apologized for the story only days after it appeared, the FBI came to Yaddo to interview the guests about Smedley. This group had recently dwindled in number and included only O'Connor, Lowell, Elizabeth Hardwick, and Edward Maisel. The four were agitated by the FBI interviews and consulted several of the Yaddo board members about Ames's administrative methods and Communist sympathies, finally issuing an ultimatum: either Ames would be removed from her post or the four remaining guests would leave. Just as O'Connor had been uneasy about the FBI interviews, she also seemed uneasy about the ultimatum. However, she must have decided that their concerns were valid because she went along with the other three remaining Yaddo guests. Seeing very little foundation for the allegations, the board chose not to fire Ames, and the remaining four guests delivered on their threat and left Yaddo on March 1, 1949. After leaving Yaddo, O'Connor was effectively removed from the controversy, but she expressed her views in letters to Betty Boyd Love, stating that the Yaddo board ignored the allegations against Ames simply to cover up their own inattention to her mismanagement of affairs at Yaddo and her association with Smedley. Despite these events, O'Connor did not seem to harbor any ill will toward Ames or anyone associated with Yaddo. Ames even invited her to return to Yaddo in 1958; O'Connor declined the invitation.[27]

While O'Connor's involvement in the Elizabeth Ames/Agnes Smedley scandal was short-lived, her disdain for the behavior of many of the guests was much more enduring. Specifically, the partying, substance abuse, drinking, and casual attitude toward sex disturbed her. When her friend Cecil Dawkins was at Yaddo in 1959, O'Connor related her experiences with this kind of behavior, advising Dawkins that the best way to endure this kind of environment was to have plenty with which to occupy herself and to not be afraid to be different from the other guests. In fact, O'Connor seemed to have more of a rapport with the staff at Yaddo than she did with her fellow artists, largely because she found the staff to be more genuine and moral than the guests.

Overall, however, O'Connor's positive experiences at Yaddo seem to far outweigh the negative. She cultivated several enduring friendships while at Yaddo, most notable being her friendship with Elizabeth Fenwick Way who was also later diagnosed with lupus. The two exchanged letters throughout O'Connor's life, many of which contain irreverent comments about their condition, such as, "I have been wondering how you and the lupus epizooticus were. Me and mine are as usual."[28] It was also during this time that O'Connor secured the literary agent she would keep for the rest of her life, Elizabeth McKee. Another artist at Yaddo recommended McKee to O'Connor, and McKee took on O'Connor as a client without delay after O'Connor contacted her. In addition, O'Connor met the man who would eventually become her publisher, Robert Giroux. Clearly, O'Connor found the surroundings at Yaddo to be conducive to the serious writer. She applauded the food, the facilities, the scenery, and the wildlife in her correspondence; and while there, she came to know several people who would remain important throughout her life.

THE BIG APPLE AND THE FIRST NOVEL

After leaving Yaddo, O'Connor moved to New York City, the hub of the literary world in the 1940s. She lived at the YWCA for several weeks and then located an apartment with the help of Elizabeth Fenwick. She was repulsed by the lifestyle of most New Yorkers, which she found to be reminiscent of the Yaddo residents, and in the summer of 1949 she moved to Ridgefield, Connecticut, into the garage apartment of Robert and Sally Fitzgerald's home in the country. She had been introduced to the Fitzgeralds only months before, but the friendship between the couple and the young writer grew rapidly, due at least in part to their strong mutual devotion to Catholicism. While living with the Fitzgeralds, O'Connor continued her practice of attending mass every morning; Robert and Sally took turns driving O'Connor to mass and staying home to watch the children. While Robert taught English at Sarah Lawrence College and Sally took care of their children, O'Connor worked on finishing her novel *Wise Blood*, occasionally babysitting the Fitzgerald children and indulging in martinis and evening conversation with the Fitzgeralds, mostly about books or about Catholicism. The three became close very quickly, and O'Connor was even asked to be Marie Juliana Fitzgerald's godmother when she was baptized in May 1950. What began was a relationship that would span O'Connor's entire life as the Fitzgeralds became and remained some of her closest friends and mentors.[29]

During this time, O'Connor also began to wrangle with Rinehart Publishing over the publication of her first novel, *Wise Blood*. McKee sent the manuscript to John Selby at Rinehart, and his response to the novel, which O'Connor felt was belated to begin with, offended O'Connor who felt as if he addressed her as a "slightly dim-witted Camp Fire Girl."[30] Selby criticized the novel for being unconventional and accused O'Connor of limiting the scope of the novel (namely, its Catholic themes set in a Protestant South) simply because her own personal experiences were limited. Since these issues went to the heart of the novel's content, O'Connor was not willing to compromise. To complicate matters, Robert Giroux, who was with Harcourt Brace at that time, offered O'Connor a $1,500 advance for the manuscript. In O'Connor's opinion, Selby wanted her to change areas of the book she was simply not willing to change, and Rinehart finally released O'Connor, giving her the freedom to submit the manuscript to Harcourt. However, the release upset her because Selby wrote a letter characterizing O'Connor as stubborn, difficult to work with, and "unethical."[31] That last word caused her a great deal of inner turbulence: she was very concerned with doing the right thing—regardless of Selby's opinion of her.

Finally, O'Connor resolved the issues she had with Selby and signed a contract with Harcourt. However, she also began to have the first of several health problems. She had surgery for Dietl's Crisis, also known as a "floating kidney," in 1949 during the Christmas holiday that she spent in Milledgeville; in this situation, a kidney moves out of place, blocking the ureter. Despite the surgery, O'Connor returned to Connecticut in 1950, but her health continued to decline. At this time, no one realized that the true nature of her illness would forever change her life.

NOTES

1. Sally Fitzgerald, "Root and Branch: O'Connor of Georgia," *Georgia Historical Quarterly* 64, no. 4 (1980): 387.

2. Lorine M. Getz, *Flannery O'Connor: Her Life, Library and Book Reviews* (New York: Edwin Mellon Press, 1980), p. 6.

3. Fitzgerald, "Root and Branch," p. 387.

4. Fitzgerald, "Root and Branch," p. 385.

5. Fitzgerald, "Root and Branch," pp. 382–86.

6. Jean W. Cash, *Flannery O'Connor: A Life* (Knoxville: University of Tennessee Press, 2002), pp. 8–10.

7. Cash, *Flannery O'Connor: A Life*, p. 13.

8. Cash, *Flannery O'Connor: A Life*, p. 16.

9. Cash, *Flannery O'Connor: A Life*, p. 18.

10. Cash, *Flannery O'Connor: A Life*, p. 43.

11. "Flannery O'Connor: Cartoonist," *Hogan's Alley: The Online Magazine of the Cartoon Arts*, http://cagle.slate.msn.com/hogan/issue 1/flannery.asp.

12. Cash, *Flannery O'Connor: A Life*, p. 71.

13. "The Life of Flannery O'Connor," http://gographics.com/funnies/flann1.htm.

14. Cash, *Flannery O'Connor: A Life*, p. 60.

15. "The Life of Flannery O'Connor," http://gographics.com/funnies/flann1.htm.

16. Cash, *Flannery O'Connor: A Life*, p. 57.

17. Betty Boyd Love, "Recollections of Flannery O'Connor," *The Flannery O'Connor Bulletin* 14 (1985): 70.

18. Cash, *Flannery O'Connor: A Life*, p. 80.

19. "Flannery O'Connor: Cartoonist," http://cagle.slate.msn.com/hogan/issue 1/flannery.asp.

20. Cash, *Flannery O'Connor: A Life*, p. 86.

21. Jean Wylder, "Flannery O'Connor: A Reminiscence and Some Letters," *North American Review* (Spring 1970): 61.

22. Cash, *Flannery O'Connor: A Life*, pp. 98–99.

23. Virginia Wray, "The Importance of Home to the Fiction of Flannery O'Connor," *Renascence* 47 (Winter 1995): 103–15.

24. Cash, *Flannery O'Connor: A Life*, p. 103.

25. Flannery O'Connor, "The Nature and Aim of Fiction," *Mystery and Manners: Occasional Prose*, ed. Sally and Robert Fitzgerald (New York: Farrar, Straus, and Giroux, 1969), p. 86.

26. "Yaddo and Flannery O'Connor," http://library.gcsu.edu/~sc/focyaddo.html.

27. Cash, *Flannery O'Connor: A Life*, pp. 113, 116–21.

28. Letter to Elizabeth Fenwick, September 13, 1956, *The Habit of Being*, ed. Sally Fitzgerald (New York: Farrar, Straus, and Giroux, 1979), p. 174.

29. Cash, *Flannery O'Connor: A Life*, pp. 123–27.

30. Letter to Elizabeth McKee, February 19, 1949, *The Habit of Being*, p. 9.

31. Fitzgerald, ed., *The Habit of Being*, p. 17.

Chapter 2

RETURN TO MILLEDGEVILLE

When O'Connor left the Connecticut home of Sally and Robert Fitzgerald in December 1950, one wonders if she thought she was visiting Milledgeville only for the holidays instead of returning for the rest of her life. When her health rapidly declined, she faced no other choice but to remain in Milledgeville—the hometown where she was known as "Mary Flannery" or as "Regina's daughter"—so that her mother could care for her. Though she was no invalid, O'Connor was most certainly a realist and recognized that if she were to continue what she felt was her life's work, she would not be able to do it alone.

O'Connor had been ill before she ever left Connecticut and had visited a doctor upon the insistence of Robert and Sally Fitzgerald. The preliminary diagnosis for the heaviness in her limbs was arthritis, but she was advised by the doctor to seek a second opinion once she arrived home in Georgia. O'Connor became terribly ill on the train ride home, and her uncle Louis Cline, who picked her up at the train station in Atlanta, was, according to Sally Fitzgerald, "horrified at her appearance.... She seemed to have become, as he said, 'a shriveled up old woman.'"[1] O'Connor was admitted to the hospital almost immediately due to a high fever, and her mother phoned the Fitzgeralds several weeks later with news of O'Connor's eminent death. However, the end was not to come yet for the 26-year-old O'Connor once she became the patient of Dr. Arthur J. Merrill, an Atlanta lupus specialist who officially diagnosed her with the disease. Surprisingly enough, Regina O'Connor kept the diagnosis a secret from O'Connor until Christmas 1952. While O'Connor was visiting the Fitzgeralds for the holidays, Sally broke the news of the diagnosis to O'Connor, knowing she was going against Regina's wishes. Never one to be less than fully attentive to the world around her, O'Connor revealed that she had suspected lupus all along and thanked Fitzgerald for her honesty.

THE RED WOLF

The lupus diagnosis must have been a difficult blow to O'Connor, her mother, and all those who knew of the death of her father. Having watched him die, O'Connor must have known full well the physical toll this chronic inflammatory disease of the immune system would take: aching joints, fatigue, skin rashes, hair loss, and numerous hospitalizations.[2] In addition to the physical effects of the disease itself—the "Red Wolf" as she called it[3]—O'Connor would have to endure the side effects of her medication which consisted largely of ACTH, a corticosteroid. These side effects included skin splotchiness, anemia, bone deterioration, tumors, constantly racing thoughts, insomnia, malfunctioning kidneys, swollen feet and face, nausea, immobility, and chronic pain.[4] O'Connor walked on crutches for the rest of her life and was forced to limit her time writing to the morning hours because of her fatigue.

Apparently realizing that her attitude toward her condition would have an enormous effect on her ability to function, she dealt with the disease in what became typical O'Connor fashion: one of stoic grace, acceptance, and even humor. After learning that she would most likely never walk without the crutches she detested, O'Connor wrote to Betty Hester, "... so much for that. I will henceforth be a structure with flying buttresses...."[5] O'Connor did not treat her illness like a big deal, and she asked that others do the same. She abhorred the uninvited pity she often received, and according to Regina O'Connor, "We never made a production out of her illness. She was just ill—and that was it."[6]

unlike   mrs Hope

MOTHER AND DAUGHTER

At the same time, O'Connor knew her limits, as did her mother. Regina was very protective of O'Connor, perhaps because she had already lost her husband to lupus and feared losing her only child. Some perceived her as tyrannical, "[giving] off an air of martyrdom which was the exact opposite of her daughter's quiet acceptance,"[7] and as a nuisance who dominated conversations, never allowing O'Connor to speak for herself. Others describe her as "the epitome of the quick-witted, hospitable southern women ... a joy to be around."[8] Regardless of these opinions, her protection of O'Connor was most surely stifling at times. For example, most 28 year olds are accustomed to making their own decisions and guiding their own lives, but in the summer of 1953, Regina forbade O'Connor from visiting Sally and Robert Fitzgerald for more than a week.

Like any woman of her age, O'Connor treasured her autonomy, despite the fact that she was technically living in her mother's house, and the conflict between O'Connor's need for independence and Regina's insistence on sheltering her and dominating her daily existence has led many to believe that the two had a hostile relationship. O'Connor irreverently referred to her mother as "Regina" or "the parent" and sought financial independence by purchasing rental property in Milledgeville, winning prizes and grants, lecturing around the country, and selling a story to television. The two lived remarkably separate lives, with Regina running the dairy farm, attending cattle auctions, baling hay, and actively laboring alongside the hired workers and O'Connor focusing on her writing and cultivating a private space within her room where she wrote. Even there her mother interfered, much to O'Connor's dismay, and, from time to time, decided to clean her room, a process that made O'Connor feel she was "being sawed in two without ether."[9]

Regina's domineering nature became almost unbearable for O'Connor when they entertained guests. Ever conscious of the social responsibilities of a "Southern lady," Regina's conversational efforts often made O'Connor, who had no use for Southern societal conventions, nervous. Regina was always very talkative when entertaining guests, and Cash asserts, "She did not seem to realize that many of them had come to see Flannery O'Connor, the writer, not Regina Cline O'Connor, the socialite and farmer."[10] While some saw her garrulousness as an appropriate attempt to draw O'Connor out socially, others, such as Fr. James McCown, saw her as intrusive and annoying: "She sat in on each conversation and invariably side-tracked it into something about the scandalous new things happening in the Church ... she considered her subjects as engrossing and important as anything Flannery talked about."[11] As O'Connor wrote to Maryat Lee after she visited Andalusia, "the parental presence never contributes to my articulateness, and I might have done better at answering some of your questions had I entertained you in the hen house...."[12] While Regina seemed to make O'Connor nervous at times, her intrusiveness did not seem to annoy O'Connor, according to McCown.

Yet there were many practical benefits of Regina's somewhat dictatorial presence in her daughter's life. Because of the lupus, O'Connor was forced to adhere to a strict schedule that allowed her to write only three hours in the morning. Regina was largely responsible for making sure those hours were uninterrupted, even going so far as to entertain guests who appeared during O'Connor's working hours out of O'Connor's hearing, and O'Connor fittingly dedicated *Wise Blood* to Regina. In addition, the move to Andalusia from the Cline mansion was largely due to Regina's concern for O'Connor's mobility, which the Cline mansion's numerous stairs did not accommodate. Andalusia was a 544-acre farm which Regina inherited jointly with her brother Louis Cline from their uncle Bernard Cline, who died in 1947. It is approximately four miles north of Milledgeville and consisted at the time of the primary residence, the home of resident farmers Jack and Louise Hill, a large barn and a small barn, a shed for equipment, a shed for milk-processing, a garage, a water tower, a horse stable, a pump house, and three tenant houses.[13] Built in the 1850s, the main house, a white, two-story structure, also contained stairs, which O'Connor was able to avoid by having her bedroom downstairs in the front of the house. An Atlanta resident, Louis Cline left management of the farm to Regina, who found success in a "man's world" of tenant farmers, cattle auctions, and dairy farming. This left O'Connor to write.

Without a doubt, the two shared an intense, abiding (if antagonistic) love for one another, perhaps because they were so different—and yet so alike. While Regina seemed to voice her opinion on every subject known to man (including O'Connor's stories), whether she understood the subject or not, O'Connor chose her words carefully and often used them sparingly. On the other hand, "both were determined, unsentimental women with none of the childlike femininity sometimes associated with Southern women of their class."[14] O'Connor even admitted that she hoped to die before her mother, saying to Sally Fitzgerald the last time the two spoke, "I don't know what I would do without her."[15]

Unquestionably, the two women existed on very different intellectual levels. O'Connor possessed, without a doubt, one of the most impressive intellects of her time, which is evidenced in her fiction, her letters, her speeches, and even her book reviews. She possessed a perceptiveness about even the most complex spiritual issues and often intimidated other writers, such as her colleagues at Iowa and poet Elizabeth Bishop, who turned down an invitation to Andalusia for this reason. Regina, on the other hand, was a skillful businesswoman who was very conscious of finances, but she did not possess the intellectual sharpness of her daughter. In a letter to Robert and Sally Fitzgerald, O'Connor recounted Regina's reading of the manuscript of *Wise Blood* and falling asleep only nine pages into it. According to Cash, Regina often inquired about the authors O'Connor read, such as Franz Kafka or Evelyn Waugh, but she was not interested in reading them herself. Although Regina clearly respected O'Connor's talent and protected the time she allotted to writing, from time to time she would express to O'Connor her dismay at the fact that O'Connor's work wasn't popular with very many people. According to a letter O'Connor wrote to Cecil Dawkins in April 1959, Regina even accused O'Connor of wasting her God-given talent, an indictment which infuriated O'Connor.

>Despite their existence on different intellectual levels and Regina's reservations about her daughter's work, Regina always supported her unwaveringly. Even when others winced at O'Connor's graphic violence and grotesque characters, Regina prompted O'Connor to ask her editor, Caroline Carver, for five copies of O'Connor's short story collection *A Good Man is Hard to Find* because Regina wanted to send them to sick friends. When Regina presented Georgia College and State University in Milledgeville with O'Connor's papers and some of her possessions in 1972, she stated, "I approved of what she did, but that was Flannery—not me. As Flannery always said, 'You run the farm and I'll run the writing.' I approve of everything she did."[16]

All in all, the move back to the South was one that O'Connor at first dreaded but later came to see as a blessing. As a young woman, she did as many young people do and sought to get as far away from home as possible, but the longer she was away from the South, the more she felt drawn to it. She may have left sick *of* the South but eventually became homesick *for* it, and the return precipitated by her lupus was a development that many feel was invaluable to her growth as a writer. At least one critic has said that her physical struggles "led her to identify with human frailty. She both judged and loved her characters. Her capacity for love and sympathy was expanded by daily experience of physical weakness."[17] According to O'Connor, "Usually the artist has to suffer certain deprivations in order to use his gift with integrity."[18] Any deprivations she experienced because of the lupus and the subsequent return to the South, she saw as the price of her gift as an artist—a small price to pay.

A BIG DECISION

While her permanent relocation to Milledgeville was largely out of O'Connor's control, other elements of her life were decidedly within her control, and in one area in particular, O'Connor appears to have made a very deliberate decision soon after her move back to Milledgeville. O'Connor's romantic attachments have been a subject of considerable scrutiny since her death, largely because she seems to have had few of them and she never married. O'Connor herself claimed in a letter to Betty Hester that she had been in love many times. However, some maintain that when she felt the physical limits placed upon her by lupus dictated a choice, she chose writing over a pursuit of a romantic relationship and, ultimately, marriage, feeling she would never be able to do both and not willing to sacrifice her art.

The years since O'Connor's death have also generated a great deal of speculation regarding her sexual orientation. While O'Connor attended single-sex schools until going to the University of Iowa, Cash claims that her brilliance and individualism also contributed to her isolation from others, both male and female, and she may have been intentionally defying the Southern belle stereotype she so detested by not actively pursuing heterosexual relationships. As previously mentioned, her talent intimidated many members of the opposite sex, especially those with whom she participated in the Writer's Workshop. O'Connor herself wrote in her personal letters that she used to "go with" Erik Langkjaer, a Harcourt Brace textbook salesman, to whom GSCW history professor Helen Greene introduced her. Greene was optimistic about the relationship but presumed it would not develop romantically because Langkjaer was not Roman Catholic. On the other hand, Sally Fitzgerald claims that O'Connor was in love with Langkjaer and that her affection was not reciprocated. Others believe she carried on a romance with Robie Macauley, as previously mentioned. Otherwise, her associations with men seemed to be platonic, which may have contributed as much to her decision to remain unmarried as did her desire to focus on her work.

This evidence considered, many maintain that O'Connor must have concealed her homosexuality, especially because of her numerous close friendships with women, several of whom were lesbians, most notably Maryat Lee. According to Cash, Lee's journal states clearly that her relationship with O'Connor was nonsexual but that Lee may have wanted a sexual relationship. On the other hand, Lee's brother Robert E. "Buzz" Lee, who was president of GSCW from 1956–1967, states that his sister had no such interest in O'Connor as a sexual partner. Maryat made fervent declarations of her love for O'Connor in several letters, which O'Connor rebuffed in pious, theological terms and which apparently hurt Lee's feelings. O'Connor later apologized for her reply and her poor sensitivity. Lee continued to be frustrated with O'Connor's rejection of her offer of love and even physical affection, which, according to Cash, signifies that O'Connor was not a lesbian and did not wish to be involved in "entangling love relationships" of any sort.[19] Ralph Wood agrees, stating that O'Connor did not marry not because she did not like men; on the contrary, she was simply busy, ill, and largely confined to home. Yet many have wondered: "so many of the better known women writers have defied sociosexual codes, and have been lesbian...."[20] So why not O'Connor?

According to Cash, this obsession with O'Connor's sexual orientation is a result of the sexual preoccupation of our society and of "jealousy and a desire to spice small-town [Milledgeville] salacious gossip."[21] As for O'Connor herself, her comments on homosexuality are few. According to Cash, she scorned a classmate who accused her of carrying on a romantic relationship with Betty Boyd Love while the two were students at GSCW, and in a letter to Betty Hester, she refers to homosexuality as an experiment of "those arty people in the Village."[22] Was O'Connor a lesbian? The evidence seems to say that she was not, but a definitive answer to this question seems to have died with her.

OUTSIDE MILLEDGEVILLE

In addition to this speculation over O'Connor's sexual orientation, a debate has raged for years regarding her contact with the world outside Milledgeville. Many have claimed she was a recluse. One writer on a frustrating search in Milledgeville for information regarding O'Connor claims that she most likely would not have wanted to be found and surely must have been lonesome since she was isolated and friendless.[23] However, nothing could have been further from the truth. Certainly her physical condition limited her excursions from Andalusia, but O'Connor relished the time she spent lecturing and traveling, entertaining visitors, spending time with friends in Milledgeville, and perhaps most of all, cultivating friendships through letters.

Despite the limitations of her illness and despite popular belief that O'Connor was a recluse, O'Connor delivered approximately 60 lectures in cities across America, primarily at colleges and universities. Not only did this give her an opportunity to refine and share her ideas on issues regarding writing, the South, and religion, but it also gave her the chance to venture away from Milledgeville and earn some money that was exclusively hers. Her first public engagements were in Milledgeville after the publication of *Wise Blood*, and as time passed, she was invited to such locations as Hollins College in Virginia; Georgetown University in Washington, D.C.; Emory University in Atlanta; the University of Chicago; Smith College in Northampton, Massachusetts (where she also received an honorary doctorate); Agnes Scott College in Decatur, Georgia; Loyola University in New Orleans; East Texas University in Commerce; and Vanderbilt University in Nashville. Apparently, O'Connor was successful in these endeavors, for she never seemed to lack invitations for speaking engagements. Of her visit to Emory in 1967, a reviewer wrote, "she was the hit of the season."[24]

Instead of presenting a new speech at every engagement, O'Connor often reworked and delivered the same material repeatedly. As much as O'Connor did not want to be shallow and falsely uplifting in her public speaking, she also didn't want to sound like an "innerluckchul," as she often referred to pretentious academics. Therefore, she worked very hard on every lecture, revising each one at least three times, even if she only delivered it once, to make sure it was clear and, again, to revise it if she were giving a previously delivered lecture. Most of these speeches were published at some point and/or collected in the volume *Mystery and Manners: Occasional Prose*. O'Connor gave one particular speech entitled "The Catholic Novelist in the Protestant South" at least 15 times.[25] In it she claims that certain essential elements of Catholic thought, such as Communion, grace, the existence of evil, and the stories of the Bible, are especially plentiful in the South because of its religious groundings, though few Catholic writers recognize that fact. O'Connor often criticized Catholic literature for its sentimentality, saying, "We Catholics are much given to the instant answer. Fiction doesn't have any.... [The author] will lift up the old lady's heart without cost to himself or her. He will forget that the devil is still at his task of winning souls and that grace cuts with the sword Christ said he came to bring."[26] According to O'Connor, Catholic writers often inhabited the realm of propaganda instead of the realm of art. In other words, O'Connor seems to have had a difficult time finding Catholic writing that presented the message of Christ in a realistic way that readers could recognize; therefore, since she could not find such writing, she produced it herself.

O'Connor presented two of her other lectures a number of times: "The Fiction Writer and His Country" and "Some Aspects of the Grotesque in Southern Fiction." "The Fiction Writer and His Country" challenges the popular notion that the Southern writer speaks only for the South and not for America as a whole. According to O'Connor, other writers had disputed this idea before her but never from the point of view of a *Christian* Southern writer. She claimed that the South was, regrettably, losing its uniqueness and becoming more and more like the rest of America, and also regrettably, the work of Southern writers was beginning to be indistinguishable from the work of writers from other regions. If writers are not accepted and appreciated for their unique, even regional, qualities, the duty of speaking for America would fall to advertising agencies, O'Connor said. Perhaps most important to remember, she claimed, was that each writer is part of a country—a geographical locale—but his country is also part of who he is—part of his identity:

> The writer's value is lost, both to himself and to his country, as soon as he ceases to see that country as a part of himself, and to know oneself is, above all, to know what one lacks.... The first product of self-knowledge is humility, and this is not a virtue conspicuous in any national character.[27]

In "Some Aspects of the Grotesque in Southern Fiction," O'Connor addressed the public's tendency to pigeonhole authors in certain "schools," particularly Southern and grotesque, and then expect the author's work to adhere to the qualities of that school, no matter how erroneous they might be. For example, O'Connor stated that readers of "Southern" writing expected her work to adhere with absolute fidelity to Southern life: "I am always having it pointed out to me that life in Georgia is not at all the way I picture it, that escaped criminals do not roam the roads exterminating families [a reference to the story "A Good Man is Hard to Find"], nor Bible salesmen prowl about looking for girls with wooden legs [a reference to the story "Good Country People"]." She specifically tackled charges that her work was unrealistic because of its reliance on the grotesque, in which "the writer has made alive some experience which we are not accustomed to observe every day, or which the ordinary man may never experience in his ordinary life."[28] She stated that each author's "realism" would depend on his or her definition of reality, and what was reality for a writer in the South, with its theological base, might not be reality for a writer or reader from the North.

More than delivering lectures, however, O'Connor enjoyed reading from her short stories, especially "A Good Man is Hard to Find." It was important to O'Connor that readers understand the themes she intended to communicate through each story, primarily that even her most "disturbing" characters are on a quest to find God and His grace in a secular world. She quickly grew impatient with well-meaning students who asked about things such as the significance of the Misfit's hat in "A Good Man is Hard to Find." O'Connor offered a terse response to this question: to cover his head. According to friend Maryat Lee, even though O'Connor was naturally a quiet person, she genuinely enjoyed speaking before groups and was gifted at doing so.

VISITORS

Despite her reputation as an aloof woman, O'Connor cherished relationships with others. Ralph Wood states that she was not able to form the close relationships that she desired, making this situation the "essential disappointment of [her] life."[29] However, when one examines the many visitors she received and the hundreds of letters she exchanged, one doubts the veracity of his assertion. While O'Connor may not have been able to travel as freely as she liked, she often entertained visitors at Andalusia. One of her most frequent visitors was Jesuit priest Fr. James McCown who became a close friend and spiritual mentor after hearing of O'Connor's work and seeking her out at Andalusia. Cash describes McCown, whose congregation was in Macon, as jovial and friendly, much unlike Milledgeville's priest and much like O'Connor. His approval of her work brought them together, and their mutual interest in literature enriched a relationship that developed over many years. They often recommended books to one another, and he helped her navigate spiritual issues she faced, from having broken Catholic dietary laws to dealing with the selections of a reading group that met at Andalusia.

This relationship also led O'Connor to others, including Tom and Louise Gossett, who were professors at Wesleyan College and Mercer University, respectively, in Macon from 1954–1958. The three maintained a friendship of casual visits, daiquiris on the front porch of Andalusia, and stops the Gossets made in Milledgeville on their way to West Virginia from San Antonio, where they relocated in 1958. According to Louise Gossett, "[W]e always stood in such awe of [O'Connor] as such a accomplished person that we never wanted to intrude on her life and her way of living. . . . Maybe one of the reasons she enjoyed our company was that we weren't making demands that she perform in a great manner."[30]

O'Connor also entertained and maintained relationships with several notable writers of her day, the best known being Katherine Anne Porter. In fact, it was the Gossets who took Porter to Andalusia in 1958. Porter and O'Connor seemed to present the ultimate contrast: Porter was a sophisticated woman of elegant dress and jewelry, while O'Connor was most often found in jeans and a sweatshirt. In fact, one element of their first conversation made the Gossets worry that the two might not get along at all: upon looking over the land at Andalusia, Porter said excitedly, "What a lovely prospect!" Upon looking at the same tract of land, O'Connor responded, "Looks like a field to me."[31]

Much to the relief of the Gossets, the two did enjoy each other's company as they discussed such issues as death, the toil of writing, and O'Connor's chickens and peafowl, with which Porter was fascinated. The two did not keep in close contact with one another, though O'Connor did send Porter a postcard from her trip to Lourdes. The two also appeared together as part of a panel discussion on Southern literature at Wesleyan College, and Porter visited Andalusia a second time. During this second visit, Porter asked about a chicken O'Connor had when Porter visited the first time two years earlier, prompting O'Connor to write, "I call that having a talent for winning friends and influencing people when you remember to inquire for a chicken that you met two years before."[32]

Among O'Connor's other author-friends was Louise Abbot. After reading *A Good Man is Hard to Find*, Abbot, a hopeful young writer and resident of Louisville, Georgia, wrote to O'Connor, asking if she could visit her at Andalusia. The two met there in 1957 and quickly learned that their families shared similar Georgia backgrounds, specifically in Savannah. The writers shared personal similarities in their senses of humor and occasional shyness and continued to meet often in Milledgeville throughout the course of O'Connor's life. Though Abbot was a member of the Associate Reformed Presbyterian Church, the two regularly discussed intimate spiritual issues. On one such occasion that Abbot confided in O'Connor about some of her spiritual doubts, O'Connor replied with a compassionate but direct response that strips any ounce of possible sentimentality from the concept of true faith: "What people don't realize is how much religion costs. They think faith is a big electric blanket, when of course it is the cross.[33]

Although O'Connor's ability to travel far from home was restricted, she found several close friends virtually in her own backyard. Among these were Rosa Lee Walston and Helen Greene, professors of English and history, respectively, at GSCW. According to Cash, these friendships allowed O'Connor to have local relationships with people who could truly appreciate her work and her intellect. O'Connor had known Greene before her departure for Iowa in 1945, and the two stayed in touch during O'Connor's absence from Milledgeville. Once O'Connor returned to Milledgeville, she and Greene often shared meals at Andalusia.

Walston joined the English faculty in 1946 and met O'Connor when she came home on a visit to Milledgeville from Iowa. Once O'Connor returned to Milledgeville for good, the relationship flourished. The two had a very casual friendship in which they got together just to enjoy each other's company and conversation. Walston also became O'Connor's strongest link to GSCW and involved her in the Literary Guild, a club for English majors, where O'Connor spoke annually and hosted an annual picnic for the group at Andalusia. Walston was in England when O'Connor died but was able to visit her in the hospital at Milledgeville before her death. The fact that O'Connor was not allowed visitors but specifically asked that Walston be allowed to see her after hearing Walston talking to Regina outside her room illustrates the cherished bond the two women shared.

LETTERS

While it is evident that O'Connor had regular contact with friends from near and far, her most extensive contact with the largest variety of people was through her letters, which were collected by Sally Fitzgerald in 1979 and published under the title *The Habit of Being*. According to Fitzgerald, the letters reveal a great deal of who O'Connor was: "There she stands to me, a phoenix risen from her own words: calm, slow, funny, courteous, both modest and very sure of herself, intense, sharply penetrating, devout but never pietistic, downright, occasionally fierce, and honest in a way that restores honor to the word."[34]

Many of the letters O'Connor received were from people whom she had not met but who had read her work, some of whom proved to be quite peculiar. However, O'Connor replied to every letter and met the strangest ones with her own unique sense of humor. For example, when a Cincinnati man wrote O'Connor a flirtatious letter, she responded to him that she wouldn't like him much but that he would be "crazy about me as I had seven gold teeth and weighed 250 pounds."[35] About some other eccentrics she received letters from, she wrote that they were just the kind of people she might have created for one of her stories but ones she would not want to get close to, except "in the imagination."[36]

Yet several of the letters she received from people she had not met led to lifelong friendships, such as the one with Louise Abbot mentioned above. However, standing above all the relationships O'Connor developed through letters is that with Betty Hester, referred to as "A" for "anonymous" in *The Habit of Being*. Hester worked as a clerk at a credit bureau in Atlanta, wrote profusely, was never published, and never married, but her intellect was of the sort that grabbed O'Connor's attention from the first letter. Their exchange of approximately 300 letters over 9 years satisfied a need for companionship for both women and helped

O'Connor solidify her own religious beliefs since many of their letters discussed O'Connor's faith.[37]

The first letter O'Connor received from Hester was after Hester had read *Wise Blood* and *A Good Man is Hard to Find* and wanted to share her evaluation of the books with O'Connor. It was clear from Hester's letter that she could truly appreciate and understand O'Connor's work. Their bond was immediate, and O'Connor replied to her letter, "The distance is 87 miles but I feel the spiritual distance is shorter." It appears that Hester may have been a bit intimidated by O'Connor at first, but O'Connor replied reassuringly to Hester by saying that her "fame" made her feel a bit ridiculous at times: "It's a comic distinction shared with Roy Rogers' horse and Miss Watermelon of 1955."[38]

While the letters between O'Connor and Hester discuss many issues, the two foremost are religion and writing. Hester expressed a strong interest in Catholicism, and O'Connor's responses to her questions give us a rich resource for understanding O'Connor's own convictions. For example, when Hester expressed her spiritual doubts, O'Connor provided responses that reveal that she too had doubts but relied on God to help her overcome them. The two also discussed such weighty issues as the Virgin birth and Incarnation of Christ, bodily resurrection after death, and the Eucharist. For example, Hester apparently believed that the Incarnation had to fulfill the believer emotionally before it could become a spiritual truth. O'Connor vehemently disagreed in a letter dated September 6, 1955, stating that most Christian truths, including the very existence of God, are not emotionally fulfilling, especially to those raised in the secular world. However, any lack of fulfillment felt on the part of the believer does not negate the fact of God's existence or the Incarnation of Christ. In another difference of opinion, Hester apparently believed that God can be judged by scientific human examination of the world; O'Connor, on the other hand, felt that human knowledge is far too limited to judge God by any standards other than his omniscience and omnipotence. The fact that Hester converted to Catholicism was a great source of joy for O'Connor; however, this joy was pierced with disappointment when Hester left the church in 1961.

Because Hester was a writer herself, she and O'Connor often traded theories about the job of the writer and critiqued each other's manuscripts. For example, when the two discussed the writer's job of conveying emotion through his or her work, O'Connor advised Hester of the power of suggestion in her writing: having something obvious happen in a story is predictable and ineffective. At the same time, O'Connor openly admitted that she was not a "subtle" writer in the tradition of Eudora Welty but instead employed the most obvious symbols—things impossible for people to miss, such as the sun. Hester also apparently believed that a writer reveals much if not all of himself or herself through his or her work, but according to O'Connor, part of the writer's job is to see that this does *not* happen because each story should be larger than any individual writer's personal qualities. While O'Connor shared with her friend the wisdom she had harvested as a writer, O'Connor also valued Hester's opinion of her work. For example, O'Connor commented on an enclosed copy of the short story "Greenleaf" that she wanted Hester's candid opinion and would not be hurt if Hester's comments were negative. At the same time, O'Connor was not shy in rebuffing Hester's opinion of her work if she felt it was invalid. For example, Hester commented that Hulga in "Good Country People" realizes her need to worship God; O'Connor maintained that Hester's view was not supported by the story itself and that the only thing Hulga realizes is that she is not as clever as she thinks she is.

Clearly, these two women shared an intimate friendship, discussing issues most dear to them, of an artistic, religious, and personal nature. Cash notes that of all the letters collected in *The Habit of Being,* only in those to Betty Hester does O'Connor confide her feelings about her father's death, stating that she had many of his imperfections but felt that, as a writer, she was able to accomplish things her father always wanted to but was never able to accomplish. Although Hester never knew Edward O'Connor, she had an aunt who had known him, a fact which may have persuaded O'Connor to discuss her father with Hester. More likely, O'Connor simply felt more safe sharing her innermost feelings with Hester than with any of her other friends or correspondents simply because the two shared a very close relationship.[39] Despite their closeness, Hester and O'Connor experienced some insecurities in their relationship, neither wanting to put an undue burden on the other with her letters. However, in just a few sentences, O'Connor was able to assure Hester of the importance of their friendship: "... my writing to you is a free act, unconnected with character, duty or compulsion ... be assured that these letters from you are something in my life."[40]

Perhaps second only to Hester in O'Connor's correspondence was New York playwright Maryat Lee. Lee seemed to be the exact opposite of O'Connor in the most important areas of her life. While O'Connor was a devoted Catholic, Lee was a social activist who put little stock in religion, and while O'Connor devoted certain hours of each day to writing, Lee could be undisciplined in her approach to her work. Nevertheless, the two felt an almost immediate bond that Lee describes in a tribute she wrote after O'Connor's death. Upon first meeting, the two strolled around the grounds of Andalusia in somewhat of an awkward situation. Lee had visited O'Connor on the suggestion of a friend but had never read O'Connor's work, leaving the two little to talk about. As they stopped by a fence, they discussed their similar Southern backgrounds, and O'Connor explained why she had returned to Milledgeville from the East. Lee writes the following:

> Her voice was more halting now, as she talked about coming home, suggesting to me that she had wrestled mightily with a morass of confusion, conflict and depression and had developed an intricate plan so that all the personal and professional problems were resolved harmoniously.... [O'Connor's] eyes opened and closed with the sunlight in her face, and, with tears in mine, the full intensity of the moment was heightened in what was not said but was accepted between us. We simply stood staring, looking, discovering, accepting a kinship based on an understanding. It was one of those moments whose special significance, emotional not intellectual, seems to have mysterious strength to endure....[41]

The two corresponded for seven years, and despite such a serious beginning to their relationship, their letters contain a type of playful, mischievous tone not found anywhere else in O'Connor's correspondence. Both women were from the deep South and had families with long histories there. In addition, both devoted themselves to their writing, though in different ways. It is these differences that helped create some of the most interesting letters in the *Habit of Being* collection. Because Lee was such a strident liberal and social activist, O'Connor played the redneck persona with her, offering such "good Georgia advice" as, "don't marry no foreigner. Even if his face is white, his heart is black."[42] They often served as devil's advocate for each other, O'Connor when the discussion concerned race and the general social climate of the South and Lee when the discussion concerned religion. The two almost always referred to each other with some sort of nickname, for instance, "Flanneryat" (a play on Maryat's name) for O'Connor or "Raybat" (a reference to Rayber in O'Connor's novel *The Violent Bear It Away*) for Lee. This kind of good-natured ribbing is found throughout their letters, a prime example being an ongoing joke regarding Lee getting O'Connor a "gift" of a tiger while on a trip to Japan. The cumulative effect of these letters is to reveal two women who were genuinely and deeply fond of each other, despite their disagreements.

While the most numerous and the most interesting of O'Connor's letters are to Hester and Lee, it is impossible to examine all of O'Connor's correspondents because she had so many. However, there are others who are worthy of note, either for the role they played in her life or for the content of the letters. O'Connor kept in touch with Sally and Robert Fitzgerald regularly and visited them whenever possible, their friendship having been forged during O'Connor's residence with them in 1949. She even dedicated her first published short story collection, *A Good Man Is Hard to Find*, to them, commenting in a letter to Sally that she and Robert were her "adopted kin," especially since many of her blood relatives might have gone "into hiding" if she had dedicated the book to them.[43] It is also interesting to note that O'Connor often mentioned her peafowl and other birds in her letters to the Fitzgeralds. She seemed to mention the birds either with her closest friends, such as the Fitzgeralds, or in superficial conversation, almost as if she knew her interest in these birds was an oddity that was useful for small talk with people she would probably never see again but was also something personal that she could share with those who already accepted her for who she was. She also discussed her lupus in her letters to the Fitzgeralds, a topic she discussed with relatively few of her correspondents. Even with the Fitzgeralds, with whom she was living when she first became gravely ill, her tone was never self-pitying but instead endlessly optimistic.

Another couple with which O'Connor kept in close correspondence was Brainard and Frances Cheney, whom she met through a mutual friend, writer Caroline Gordon Tate. Brainard Cheney favorably reviewed *Wise Blood* for *Shenandoah*, a student magazine published at Washington and Lee University, and after being encouraged to do so by Tate, O'Connor wrote to Cheney regarding his review. The Cheneys had also recently converted to Roman Catholicism, giving the three another level of commonality which they were able to explore when the Cheneys stopped by Andalusia in 1953 on their way from Nashville, where they lived, to their property in southern Georgia. O'Connor visited them often, and according to Cash, they were the only people O'Connor visited on a regular basis in the late 1950s and early 1960s who did not live in Milledgeville. As with most of her close relationships, O'Connor shared her work with Brainard Cheney, while she critiqued his work as well.

As a result of her friendship with the Cheneys, O'Connor also came to know two other men with whom she corresponded regularly. Ashley Brown, a Catholic who eventually became an English professor at the University of South Carolina, became acquainted with O'Connor's work and wrote her to ask if she might like to publish one of her stories in *Shenandoah*, for which he was faculty advisor. The two became fast friends, and Brown spent a great deal of time at Andalusia, describing his time there as very relaxed. Apparently, the two shared the kind of easy friendship in which two people do not feel pressured to entertain one another but simply enjoy one another's company. The second friend she acquired through the Cheneys was Thomas Stritch, a "cradle Catholic" whose family's role in establishing the Roman Catholic Church in Georgia was more prominent than O'Connor's. The two met in 1957 when O'Connor spoke at the University of Notre Dame, where Stritch taught. As with most of her friends, O'Connor and Stritch exchanged letters centered on matters of personal and literary interests, and he visited her several times at Andalusia. After Stritch read *The Violent Bear It Away*, O'Connor was clearly pleased with his favorable reaction, writing to him that the opinions of some people were irrelevant to her but that a "certain glint" was added when he liked her work.[44] O'Connor even intended to dedicate a book to Stritch, after dedicating her next one to her uncle Louis Cline, but she died before being able to do so.

One of many writers who, like Betty Hester, sought out O'Connor after reading her work was Cecil Dawkins. Once again, kindred spirits seem to have found each other in the two Catholic writers. At the time of their first exchange of letters, Dawkins was teaching at Stephens College in Missouri and told O'Connor that she was teaching her stories to first year students, which excited O'Connor, especially since she felt her own education in contemporary authors had been lacking. As with most of O'Connor's regular correspondents, the two evaluated each other's work, discussed issues such as their personal writing habits, and discussed their faith. Dawkins struggled with her faith and with her Southern background. These struggles prompted O'Connor to encourage Dawkins to hold fast to the faith and to read some of the Catholic theologians and novelists whose work had strengthened O'Connor's faith; eventually, however, Dawkins did leave the church.[45] O'Connor also encouraged her to embrace her Southern heritage, despite its disadvantages, instead of shunning it, reminding Dawkins that her Southern heritage was part of her identity. O'Connor reminded Dawkins that she, too, had once tried to flee the South, only to return and write her best work. The two grew closer as time passed, and Dawkins was devastated at O'Connor's death: "I thought the only consciousness that ever saw from the same place in the universe that my consciousness saw from was gone. I had never felt so alone."[46]

Finally, several other writers whom O'Connor befriended through letters enabled her to remain connected to the "literary world," a function that her relationship with Maryat Lee also served. Most prominent in this area were Ted Spivey and William Sessions. Like Maryat Lee, Spivey was very different from O'Connor and gave her someone with whom to argue. For example, Spivey was greatly interested in modern psychology, but O'Connor, who always looked at life theologically, distrusted the likes of Sigmund Freud and Carl Jung. She was especially unsettled by what she felt was Spivey's misinterpretation of *The Violent Bear It Away*, which was based on their differing views of Eucharist symbolism in the book, but they always seemed able to agree to disagree. After Spivey married, their relationship abated a bit because O'Connor felt it would have been improper for him to visit her at that point, but the two always valued the intellectual stimulation their relationship provided.

O'Connor shared a similar friendship with William Sessions, who was teaching at West Georgia College when he reviewed *A Good Man is Hard to Find* in 1956. O'Connor wrote to him, the two met when he was in Milledgeville on academic business, and O'Connor invited him to visit Andalusia. Like Spivey, Sessions was also interested in modern psychology, and his Freudian sexual interpretation of *The Violent Bear It Away* unnerved O'Connor. According to critic Suzanne Morrow Paulson, O'Connor especially distrusted Freudian readings of her work, but she did not totally disallow them. Paulson writes that O'Connor's characters frequently "suffer internal conflicts because of their own narcissism and regressive behavior. O'Connor might substitute the word 'pride' for narcissism and think of regressive behavior as the sign of a spiritually underdeveloped soul."[47] At the same time, whether O'Connor wanted to admit it or not, her ways of interpreting human behavior were similar to Freud's. Yet, as Paulson notes, she was selective in whom she allowed to interpret her work in a Freudian fashion, and she wrote to Sessions that she hoped he would "get over the kind of thinking that sees in every door handle a phallic symbol.... You ain't in Manhattan."[48] The two kept in touch throughout O'Connor's life and critiqued each other's work; Sessions often visited her at Andalusia, and O'Connor visited him when she could, such as when she and her mother went to Lourdes while Sessions was living in Europe. Regina O'Connor especially liked Sessions, and she was asked to be the godmother of Sessions's and his wife's son Andrew in 1962. Sessions was also good friends with Betty Hester up until her death.

Clearly, O'Connor's life was altered forever when her body was attacked by lupus. Knowing what her future would be, she did not retreat into Andalusia in Emily Dickinson style to await the end but instead decided to do what she could with the time she had, however long that might be. Knowing that her return South was unavoidable, she battled the decision and then embraced it and, overall, was grateful for her mother's care for her. When her physical condition allowed her to travel and lecture, she did. When she felt up to entertaining visitors, she invited and welcomed them. And she wrote letters unceasingly, up until just a few days before her death. As a result, the lives of many were enriched by her ideas about writing, religion, and other issues, and her life was enriched by those with whom she corresponded. Perhaps more than anything, these letters open a timeless window into the person O'Connor was. As Robert Coles has written, "In a sense, the letters argue silently for Flannery O'Connor as a character in a novel—a person whose apparently hum-drum daily life, plainly more confined than most, is no match at all for the dramatic surges of her intellect and her soul both. What her body could not manage was more than balanced by the energies of her mind and heart."[49]

NOTES

1. Sally Fitzgerald, unpublished lecture, Converse College, April 3, 1982. Quoted in Wray, "The Importance of Home to the Fiction of Flannery O'Connor." *Renascence* 47 (Winter 1995): 1.

2. Lupus Foundation of America, http://www.lupus.org/.

3. Padgett Powell, "Andalusia is Open," *Oxford American* (July/August 2003): 30.

4. Jennifer H. Proffitt, "Lupus and Corticosteroid Imagery in the Works of Flannery O'Connor," *The Flannery O'Connor Bulletin* 26–27 (1998–2000): 77, 79, 80, 83.

5. Letter to "A," April 7, 1956, *The Habit of Being*, ed. Sally Fitzgerald (New York: Farrar, Straus, and Giroux, 1979), p. 151.

6. Margaret Shannon, "The World of Flannery O'Connor," *Atlanta Journal and Constitution Magazine*, February 20, 1972, p. 9.

7. Richard Gillman, "On Flannery O'Connor," *New York Review of Books*, August 21 1969, pp. 24–26. Rpt. in *Conversations with Flannery O'Connor*, ed. Rosemary M. Magee. (Jackson: University Press of Mississippi, 1987), p. 56.

8. "Regina O'Connor, mother of author, dies here at age 99," *Union-Recorder* (Milledgeville, GA), May 9, 1995.

9. Letter to "A," May 19, 1956, *The Habit of Being*, pp. 158–59.

10. Jean W. Cash, *Flannery O'Connor: A Life* (Knoxville: University of Tennessee Press, 2002), p. 166.

11. James H. McCown, "Remembering Flannery O'Connor." *America*, September 8, 1979, p. 86.

12. Letter to Maryat Lee, January 9, 1957, *The Habit of Being*, p. 195.

13. "Background Information About Andalusia," http://www.andalusia-farm.org/bgandalusia.htm.

14. Robert Bain and Joseph M. Flora, *Fifty Southern Writers After 1900: A Bio-Bibliographical Sourcebook* (New York: Greenwood Press, 1987), p. 336.

15. Sally Fitzgerald, Introduction to *The Habit of Being*, p. xii.

16. Shannon, "The World of Flannery O'Connor," p. 9.

17. Suzanne Morrow Paulson, *Flannery O'Connor: A Study of the Short Fiction* (Boston: Twayne, 1988), p. xi.

18. Flannery O'Connor, Address, Georgia State College for Women, January 7, 1960.

19. Cash, *Flannery O'Connor: A Life*, pp. 142–43.

20. Elizabeth A. Meese, *Crossing the Double-Cross: The Practice of Feminist Criticism* (Chapel Hill: University of North Carolina Press, 1986), p. 121.

21. Cash, *Flannery O'Connor: A Life*, pp. 138–39.

22. Letter to "A," February 1, 1957, *The Habit of Being*, p. 202.

23. Linda McGovern, "A Good Writer is Hard to Find: The Search for Flannery O'Connor," *Literary Traveler*, http://www.literarytraveler.com/summer/south/oconnor.htm.

24. Celestine Sibley, "Baboons Differ with Giraffes," *Atlanta Constitution* February 13, 1954, p. 24.

25. Cash, *Flannery O'Connor: A Life*, pp. 259–60.

26. Flannery O'Connor, "The Catholic Novelist in the Protestant South," *Collected Works*, ed. Sally Fitzgerald (New York: Library of America, 1988), pp. 863–64.

27. Flannery O'Connor, "The Fiction Writer and His Country," *Mystery and Manners: Occasional Prose*, ed. Sally and Robert Fitzgerald (New York: Farrar, Straus, and Giroux, 1969), p. 35.

28. O'Connor, "Some Aspects of the Grotesque in Southern Fiction," *Collected Works*, pp. 814–15.

29. Ralph C. Wood, *The Comedy of Redemption: Christian Faith and Comic Vision in Four American Novelists* (Notre Dame, IN: University of Notre Dame Press, 1988), p. 80.

30. Quoted in Cash, *Flannery O'Connor: A Life*, p. 185.

31. Quoted in Cash, *Flannery O'Connor: A Life*, p. 188.

32. Quoted in Cash, *Flannery O'Connor: A Life*, pp. 189–90.

33. Letter to Louise Abbot, undated Saturday, 1959, *The Habit of Being*, p. 354.

34. Sally Fitzgerald, Introduction, *The Habit of Being*, p. xii.

35. Paul Gray, "Letters of Flannery O'Connor," review of *The Habit of Being*, by Flannery O'Connor, *Time* 5 Mar. 1979, p. 86.

36. Letter to Maryat Lee, November 14, 1959, *The Habit of Being*, p. 359.

37. Joel Groover, "Author O'Connor's Correspondent Dies," *Atlanta Journal-Constitution*, December 30, 1998, p. B1.

38. Letters to "A," July 20 and August 2, 1955, *The Habit of Being*, pp. 91, 126.

39. Cash, *Flannery O'Connor: A Life*, p. 221.

40. Letter to "A," April 21, 1956, *The Habit of Being*, pp. 152–53.

41. Maryat Lee, "Flannery, 1957," *The Flannery O'Connor Bulletin* 5 (Autumn 1976): 41–42.

42. Letter to Maryat Lee, June 16, 1964, *The Habit of Being,* p. 209.

43. Letter to Sally Fitzgerald, December 26, 1954, *The Habit of Being,* p. 74.

44. Letter to Thomas Stritch, April 1960, *The Habit of Being,* p. 388.

45. Cash, *Flannery O'Connor: A Life,* pp. 240–42.

46. Quoted in Cash, *Flannery O'Connor: A Life,* p. 243.

47. Paulson, *Flannery O'Connor,* p. 6.

48. Letter to William Sessions, September 13, 1960, The *Habit of Being,* p. 407.

49. Robert Coles, "Flannery O'Connor: Letters Larger than Life," *Flannery O'Connor Bulletin* 8 (Autumn 1979): 6.

Chapter 3

THE CALLED PROPHET

Always fiercely focused and independent, once O'Connor settled into Milledgeville, she set herself to the task of writing, a mission to which she devoted herself wholly and felt she was called to fulfill. O'Connor wrote to Eileen Hall, book page editor for the diocesan paper *The Bulletin*, that she was at first concerned that her writing would be viewed as "scandalous"; while this assessment of her work did indeed surface, her concern about it was short-lived. She also did not concern herself with the expectations others had of her as a Catholic writer or a Southern writer and instead focused on her work as God's instrument. Many Northern intellectuals preferred to focus on her unconventional behavior, ignoring her strident Catholicism "so long as the crazy lady with the peacocks could tell a good story."[1] O'Connor felt that many readers and critics from all parts of the country and all ways of life misunderstood her portrayal of religious issues and of the South altogether, and when she accepted the Georgia Writers' Association Scroll for her novel *The Violent Bear It Away*, she bluntly stated, "For no matter how favorable all the critics in New York City may be, they are an unreliable lot, as incapable now as on the day they were born of interpreting Southern literature to the world."[2] In an effort to make sure her work was exactly the way *she* wanted it, O'Connor often worked and reworked her stories. According to her mother, she worked on *Wise Blood* for around five years, and over 1,000 manuscript pages have been found, even though the published book is fairly short.[3] Perhaps the best example is her short story "The Geranium," which was part of her MFA thesis at the University of Iowa. It must have been a story that she felt was very important to the focus of her work since she wrestled with it her entire life, reworking it with a new title, "An Exile in the East," and ultimately completing a final version entitled "Judgment Day" which was published in her last story collection, *Everything That Rises Must Converge*.

Because O'Connor felt the emphasis of her work was so important, she did not like for attention to be focused on *her*. After being interviewed on television in 1955, O'Connor wrote to Robie Macauley with typical self-deprecating humor that she would be glad for her television exposure to end since children around the nation were most likely watching her "glacial glare" while anxiously waiting to watch *Batman*.[4] Because she wanted her work to be the center of attention, she became exasperated when the integrity of a story was changed in an anthology or for a television program. In 1956, for example, a televised version of "The Life You Save May Be Your Own" starring Gene Kelly aired and had Tom Shiftlet *befriend* Lucynell Crater, rather than marry her in order to steal her mother's car, as he does in O'Connor's story. She reacted to Harcourt Brace editor Denver Lindley that she disliked the televised version of her story a great deal but was not as dismayed by it as she was by having to endure the fervent praise from Milledgeville residents who thought the televised version was much better than the original story.[5] In another instance, when an anthology omitted the last paragraph of this same story, friend De Vene Harold described O'Connor as "sputtering-irritated."[6]

THE COURT OF PUBLIC OPINION

As with any writer, O'Connor experienced her share of both positive and negative reviews for her novels and short story collections. After publishing several of her short stories in magazines, O'Connor published her first major work in 1952 with her novel *Wise Blood*. Reviews of the novel were mixed. *Newsweek* magazine hailed it for its creative power, while William Goyen of the *New York Times Book Review* called the characters "ill-tempered" and "one dimensional" and called O'Connor's style sensationalistic and "as direct and uncompounded as the order to a firing squad to shoot a man against a wall."[7] Joe Lee Davis remarked that the influence of such writers as Evelyn Waugh, Raymond Chandler, and Erskine Caldwell in O'Connor's artistic development were painfully evident. Davis claims that she was not a mature enough writer to nurture such influences into her own distinct style, though he did credit her with making "a good run for the money."[8]

The reviews of *Wise Blood* frustrated her editor, Robert Giroux, who said that reviewers "recognized her power but missed her point."[9] Apparently, the reviewers were not the only ones who missed her point, for her family and childhood friends were initially excited by O'Connor's success, taking pride in one they knew publishing a book and becoming famous. Then, they read the book itself. In particular, O'Connor's aunt Katie Semmes read it and had to stay in bed for a week. In addition, Semmes sent several copies to local Catholic clergy before reading the book herself and later wrote them letters of apology because of the "outrageous" content. Perhaps just as interesting were the marketing techniques used in the Signet paperback version of the novel when it was issued in 1953. The phrase "A Searching Novel of Sin and Redemption" appears on the cover, along with a picture of a man lying in a field in front of a shack while a woman removes his hat. As Sarah J. Foder notes, "This titillating scene of hillbilly sex in the field targets a mass audience" and promotes the book as a "steamy dime novel."[10]

Of course, anyone who has read the novel knows that it is anything but a steamy dime novel of backwoods romance. In *Wise Blood*, Hazel Motes has just returned from World War II and begins a spiritual quest prompted by haunting memories of his highly religious grandfather and mother. Claiming that "Nothing matters but that Jesus don't exist" and "I don't believe in sin," he takes up with prostitute Leora Watts, simpleminded peeping tom Enoch Emery, and phony and supposedly blind street preacher Asa Hawks and his daughter, Sabbath Lily. In an angry response to Hawks' hypocritical shouts of "Repent!" Haze becomes a street preacher himself and founds his own church, the Church Without Christ, because "nothing matters but that Jesus was a liar." He eventually kills another phony street preacher and, afterward, tortures himself "repentantly" before dying. Many of O'Connor's readers wondered how a "nice girl" such as O'Connor would have come up with such a story line and the profanity (including many uses of God's name) that comes with it. When Haze cries out to a crowd, "What do I need with Jesus? I got Leora Watts," many of her readers must have shuddered, especially if they were unable to separate O'Connor from her characters.[11] Cash appears to know the source of O'Connor's material: "Obviously, this 'sheltered Southern girl' had opened her senses to a world beyond the protected shell of her early upbringing, and yet incorporated the genuine spirituality of her Catholic faith to give her grotesque regionalism a universal dimension."[12] Unfortunately, many readers missed this dimension.

In 1955, O'Connor published her first short story collection, *A Good Man is Hard to Find*, which contains such famous stories as "The Life You Save May Be Your Own," "The Artificial Nigger," and "Good Country People," as well as the title story. When this collection was published,

O'Connor encountered reviews similar to those she received for *Wise Blood*. One of the most favorable reviews states that "Miss O'Connor does not always dip her pen in acid. But she does dip it in the well of uncompromising truth, leaving the human soul naked as it will be at the Judgment, face to face with God."[13] As always, some reviewers were not as generous. A *Time* magazine reviewer called the stories "witheringly sarcastic" and written in a style "as balefully direct as a death sentence." This reviewer even went as far as to refer to O'Connor as "Ferocious Flannery."[14] On the other hand, it seems that many readers of this collection understood her intentions more so than they understood *Wise Blood*, for it was after reading this collection that young writers Louise Abbot, Robert Drake, Cecil Dawkins, and others contacted her and became her regular correspondents. This collection also seemed to solidify her reputation as an important writer, and as early as 1961, "A Good Man is Hard to Find" was included in the college literary anthology *American Literary Record*. At the same time, this collection, like *Wise Blood*, was marketed to the general public in a sensationalistic way. In a scene loosely based on "Good Country People," the cover portrays a man wearing a dark suit who "reaches a clawlike hand over the foregrounded shoulder and breast of a semireclining voluptuous woman" who has begun to undress; a pitchfork and a suitcase with alcohol in it are also part of the scene.[15] No indication is made of Hulga's Ph.D. or her artificial leg, and the way the man on the cover is dressed is not even close to the description of Manley Pointer.

In 1960, O'Connor published *The Violent Bear It Away*, and again, reviews ranged from favorable to disdainful. In this, O'Connor's second novel, the orphan Francis Marion Tarwater (also known as Young Tarwater) has been raised by his great-uncle Mason Tarwater (also known as Old Tarwater), a backwoods prophet who foretells that Young Tarwater will follow in his footsteps, become a prophet, and baptize Bishop, the mentally-retarded son of his cousin. Young Tarwater fights an intense inner battle throughout the book: should he follow the "call" of his great-uncle, or should he follow the "call" of Rayber, who summons him into the modern, humanistic world? Ultimately, Young Tarwater is fighting the age-old battle between good and evil, with the devil on one shoulder and an angel on the other, figuratively speaking. The novel's title is taken from Matthew 11:12: "From the days of John the Baptist until now, the kingdom of heaven suffereth violence, and the violent bear it away." True to form and to the title, violent events in the novel result in a spiritual awakening for Young Tarwater and the ultimate end of his inner conflict: he drowns Bishop while baptizing him, and he encounters a stranger who picks him up as he is hitchhiking, drugs him, rapes him, and abandons him in the woods. After setting fire to the woods, Young Tarwater "knew that he could not turn back now. He knew that his destiny forced him on to a final revelation ... [his eyes] looked as if, touched with a coal like the lips of the prophet [Isaiah], they would never be used for ordinary sights again." After returning briefly to the home he shared with Old Tarwater, he "set toward the dark city, where the children of God lay sleeping," ready to become the prophet his great-uncle predicted he would be.[16]

According to critic Marsh Maslin, readers would not find "conventional sweetness" in The Violent Bear It Away, which would dismay many of them, but they would find "power and imagination."[17] B. J. Morgan called it the "most exciting work of American fiction since World War II."[18] Of course, not all reviews were as complimentary. Citing the characters as unrealistic and odd, Donald Davidson claimed the book belonged to an "arbitrary world of fantasy."[19] Vivian Mercier tended to agree, stating that after a person stopped reading the book, he or she would find it plausible "only if set in a dream world ... ultimately, I felt cheated."[20] Others claimed the book was about nothing more than "Tennessee hillbillies" and that "the literary South has traveled a long way from the scent of the magnolia tree to the stench of the manure pile, but in each case the stereotypes are there and the distortions persist."[21] A Time magazine reviewer conveyed a condescending attitude toward O'Connor herself, calling her a "retiring, bookish spinster who dabbles in the variants of sin and salvation like some self-tutored backwoods theologian."[22]

O'Connor would not live to see other volumes of her stories published, but Everything That Rises Must Converge (1965), which contains such stories as "A View of the Woods," "Revelation", "Parker's Back," "The Lame Shall Enter First," and the title story, was published posthumously and enjoyed mostly positive reviews, even from publications such as Time and New Yorker, which had previously disparaged or dismissed her work. Most of the favorable reviews remarked on her discernment and ability to communicate her religious message without sermonizing. A Time review especially praised her command of the language, calling her "a verbal magician whose phrases flamed like matches in the dark revealing a face in a flash ... a life in a single insight."[23] The negative reviews largely claimed that her work did not deal with universal issues but only with Christianity, the South, and dysfunctional families, making it terribly predictable and repetitive. In particular, Irving Howe cited the collection's "insecurity of tone," especially as O'Connor employs irony in the stories.[24] Mystery and Manners (1969), The Complete Stories (1971), and The Habit of Being (1979) were also published posthumously. By the time of her death, O'Connor's reputation as a serious writer was so established that the covers of her books, especially her fiction, were not as lurid and sex-centered as before. One must also wonder if her death influenced publishers to be a bit more reverent in their depiction of her work on the covers of her books. For example, *Everything That Rises Must Converge* simply bore O'Connor's name and the title on the cover and comments from writer Thomas Merton on the back.

In addition to criticism from the literary world, O'Connor had to deal with reactions closer to home: from Milledgeville residents and from Catholic readers. Many residents from her hometown failed to see beyond her identity as "Mary Flannery, Regina Cline's daughter" to the creative genius she was. This identity and O'Connor's gender carried with it certain expectations that her work violated, and the conservative nature of Milledgeville as a whole did O'Connor no favors. According to Sarah Gordon, O'Connor scholar and emeritus professor of English at Georgia College and State University (formerly Georgia State College for Women), many of the characters and violent images in O'Connor's stories upset her local readers, prime examples being the Misfit's slaughter of the grandmother and her family in "A Good Man is Hard to Find" and Mary Fortune Pitts and her grandfather beating each other to death in "A View of the Woods." Many readers seemed incapable of separating the personal convictions of O'Connor from the convictions and behaviors of her characters. For instance, Gordon recounts the story of an autograph party in Milledgeville upon the publication of *Wise Blood*. Several women who attended the party were appalled at its content, wondered how O'Connor was familiar with the people and lifestyles portrayed since "she's always associated with her own kind of people," and reportedly burned several of the books in the backyard.[25]

One might think that the response of Catholic readers would be an even greater concern to O'Connor since her faith was central to nearly every story she penned. However, she saw the work of most Catholic writers as maudlin and unrealistic, claiming that "if [a writer] is going to show the supernatural taking place, he has nowhere to do it except on the literary level of natural events, and that if he doesn't make these natural things believable in themselves, he can't make them believable in any of their spiritual extensions."[26] As a result, O'Connor's fiction is centered around commonplace events and locations: a barn; a gray, "high rat colored" car;[27] a conversation around a dinner table; a family vacation; a carnival; a "toast colored" hat;[28] and a bus ride—all of which fix her stories in the real, recognizable world.

O'Connor attributed many of the negative reactions she received from Catholic readers to their weak faith, their laziness, and their being too busy looking for something "obscene" to see that it is often the works they consider obscene that are "permeated with a Christian spirit."[29] As Richard Oxman has noted, "The pleasantness of politically correct respectability has zero to do with man's need for redemption in Flannery's eyes."[30] According to O'Connor, most Catholic readers are actually looking for "raw Instant Uplift," not the truth about the world, about God's grace, or about their need for it. O'Connor rebelled against this kind of sentimentality, claiming that unthinking Catholic readers advanced the "large body of pious trash" that she felt made up the bulk of work from Catholic writers.[31] She realized that some readers were looking for the moment of grace but many times did not find it because they were looking in the wrong places for the wrong things.

Not all Catholics were as lazy as O'Connor described them, of course. Fr. James McCown certainly read her work thoughtfully. In addition, when O'Connor died, Paul Halliman, the Archbishop of Atlanta, acknowledged that those who read her work "found a world that was often violent and apparently repulsive. To doctor it, to render it 'pretty,' to have the tale 'come out right' would have been a falsification. . . . She scorned the novelist's tricks of shock for the sake of shock, as she scorned sweetness for the sake of sweetness."[32] At least a few Catholics "got it" as O'Connor intended her readers to do.

HUMOR AND UNDERSTANDING

Despite a career's worth of many negative reviews, some downright vicious, O'Connor met her negative critics with the searing, wry humor that was simply part of her personality and was cited in many of the positive reviews of her work. For example, in a 1960 interview, she told the story of "some old lady [who] said that my book left a bad taste in her mouth. I wrote back to her and said, 'You weren't supposed to eat it.'"[33] While such flippant comments often neutralized serious criticism, much of the humor in O'Connor's work relies on some aspect of reality that is crucial to a character's life but may also be appalling and even gruesome. According to Rebecca Butler, this aspect of O'Connor's work allowed her to fight the sentimentality she saw as a plague on literature, especially Catholic literature. In addition, Butler notes that O'Connor relies on "one of Comedy's oldest purposes—that of dispelling illusion." In fact, characters' false views of reality are often made known to them by some kind of "horrifyingly repugnant reality."[34] We see this pattern repeatedly in O'Connor's work, though some realities are more horrifying than others. For example, no one would dispute that the circumstances under which the Grandmother in "A Good Man is Hard to Find" learns that she is not good as she thinks she is are much different than the circumstances under which Hulga Hopewell or Ruby Turpin learns the same lesson. Certainly, having one's family murdered before one's eyes and then being murdered oneself is much more horrific and gruesome than having one's wooden leg stolen in a barn or being hit in the head with a book thrown by an angry, offended college girl. Still, the pattern is the same, and regardless of the specific circumstances, these women's counterfeit views of themselves are exposed. All three stories are terribly humorous in places, and all three women are indeed faced with a reality that is "deeply serious or horrifyingly repugnant," at least to them: not only are they not superior to the rest of humanity, but in many ways, they are inferior to the rest of humanity or at least on the same level with it.

While these concerns are related to predominant themes in O'Connor's work, she also incorporates humor into her stories in many seemingly small but very significant ways. First, she was fond of using charactonyms, names that reflect a character's personality or temperament. For example, in "Good Country People," the phallic nature of the name "Manley Pointer" fits well with the contents of Manley's hollow Bibles—pornographic playing cards and condoms—and Mrs. Hopewell's name could not be more appropriate since her clichéd speech often reflects her eternal optimism about people. The character Tom T. Shiftlet in "The Life You Save May Be Your Own" also has an appropriate name as he is certainly a "shifty" man who manages to swindle Lucynell Crater out of her car in exchange for marrying her mentally retarded daughter whom he later abandons at a diner. In "Revelation," we know little about the Wellesley college student Mary Grace who throws a book at Ruby Turpin, except that she appears to be quiet and bookish and becomes highly agitated at the racist conversation her mother, Claud and Ruby Turpin, and the "white trash" carry on in the doctor's office. Therefore, we cannot verify for certain whether her name reveals anything about her temperament; she may in fact be yet another bitter intellectual, in the same category as Hulga Hopewell and Julian from "Everything that Rises Must Converge." However, the name "Mary Grace" is one often taken by nuns, and the name certainly helps illuminate this girl's function in the story since both the book and the epithet "wart hog from hell" that she hurls at Ruby serve as the catalyst for Ruby's journey toward realizing her need for grace. Often, O'Connor uses names in an ironic way, as with Mrs. Cope in "A Circle in the Fire." In many ways, Mrs. Cope does not "cope" very well with her life as a farmwoman as she is constantly worried about someone setting fire to her woods. Likewise, Mary Fortune Pitts does not have good fortune but instead ends up "in the pits," as she and her grandfather argue over the land on which her family lives and eventually beat each other to death. Finally, Sheppard in "The Lame Shall Enter First" fails as a shepherd as his "sheep" Rufus Johnson refuses to be guided by him, and Norton, the son who wants to be guided, is rejected by the shepherd.

In addition to character-revealing or ironic names, O'Connor was also prone to including incongruous images in her stories. For example, when the Grandmother and her family first encounter Red Sammy Butts in "A Good Man is Hard to Find," he is working underneath an automobile outside his barbeque establishment. That in itself is not necessarily odd, but the fact that a monkey is chained to a nearby chinaberry tree is not exactly what one would expect to see outside of a Southern barbeque restaurant. Even the cause of the car accident later in the story is filled with an absurd humor as the Grandmother's cat, Pitty Sing, is startled, jumps on to Bailey's shoulder, and "[clings] to his neck like a caterpillar."[35] As Lucynell Crater offers Tom Shiftlet her car in which to sleep in "The Life You Save May Be Your Own" and Shiftlet pontificates about how "the monks of old slept in their coffins," Lucynell responds, "They wasn't as advanced as we are."[36] Such a comment might be seen as sarcasm from the character, but we have become acquainted enough with the Craters in the previous paragraphs to know that Lucynell's intellect most likely makes her incapable of sarcasm because she and her daughter, also named Lucynell, are truly *not* advanced but are quite backward. The image later in the story of the daughter Lucynell picking the cherries off the hat she wore in her wedding and throwing them out the window as Shiftlet supposedly drives them to their honeymoon destination brings a smile to the reader's face as well. In "A Late Encounter with the Enemy," the image of John Wesley Poker Sash in his Boy Scout uniform wheeling General Sash around campus at breakneck speed is funny because his behavior would be typical for a 10-year-old boy but does not suit the gravity of the situation. The final scene of the boy with the dead General waiting in line at the Coke machine is just as ludicrous, as is the scene in "Parker's Back" in which Parker crashes the tractor he's driving into the only tree in the entire field, or when Sarah Ruth pushes him so hard inside his truck that he knocks the door off and lands on the ground. This second image is not necessarily humorous in itself, especially since the reader knows Sarah Ruth is very religious and Parker has just insinuated that they do not have to be married to have sex; however, O'Connor creates a humorous situation by immediately following up Parker's resolution that he "would have nothing to do with her" with a mere statement of fact: "They were married in the County Ordinary's office because Sarah Ruth thought churches were idolatrous."[37] In many of these situations, we know we probably should not laugh, but we can hardly help ourselves.

In addition, O'Connor often employs clichéd speech in her stories to add a humorous element. The most striking example is the overly positive Mrs. Hopewell, whose speech is littered with clichés such as "Nothing is perfect," "That is life," and "I always said so myself."[38] In addition, the reader may sense that Mary Grace has "thrown the book" at Ruby Turpin in "Revelation" as she condemns Ruby with the literal throwing of a book. The title "A Good Man is Hard to Find" also shows O'Connor's ingenious use of clichés, especially since the title takes on a dark, ironic meaning once the Grandmother and her family encounter the Misfit and his henchmen. Also in this story, Red Sammy Butts speaks in such clichés as "These days you don't know who to trust" and "Ain't that the truth?"[39] Ruby Turpin uses a cliché to make herself believe that she has a favorable attitude toward blacks. However, when the cliché "It's all kinds of them just like it's all kinds of us" is preceded by "There's a heap of things worse than a nigger"[40] and other bigoted remarks she makes, we see a cliché at work in its finest way in O'Connor's work: as empty speech that says very little but reveals a great deal about the character who says it. In this case, we see that Ruby Turpin says a great deal about charity and tolerance, but her inner thoughts, and in this case even her verbal comments, expose her pride and bigotry.

O'Connor also uses what Butler calls "verbal dueling," a situation in which common, often incorrect speech is paired with proper, sophisticated speech, to create a humorous effect. This sort of exchange happens several times in "The Life You Save May Be Your Own" as Shiftlet philosophizes on everything from the nature of man to open heart surgery to Lucynell the mother when all she is concerned about is where he came from and whether he is married. The conversation between Tom Shiftlet and the boy he picks up on the side of the road at the end of the story is also instructive. Shiftlet delivers a lengthy discourse on the nature of motherhood, commenting that "a boy's mother ... taught him his first prayers at her knee, ... give him love when no other would," and that his mother was "an angel of Gawd," and the young hitchhiker responds with, "You go to the devil! ... My old woman is a flea bag and yours is a stinking pole cat!"[41] The same sort of thing happens in "A Circle in the Fire" when Mrs. Cope admonishes Mrs. Pritchard, "Think of all we have. Lord, ... we have everything," and Mrs. Pritchard responds, "All I got is four abscess teeth."[42] Once again in "The Lame Shall Enter First," Sheppard patiently explains to Rufus Johnson, "It's perfectly possible that you, Rufus Johnson, will go to the moon," and Rufus responds, "I ain't going to the moon and get there alive, ... and when I die I'm going to hell."[43]

O'Connor knew that many readers would neither understand nor appreciate her humor, and she recognized that critical acclaim or even understanding of her work was probably going to come slowly. However, she felt it was worth waiting for and would not adhere to any standards other than her own. As she said in an address at GSCW in 1960,

> When I sit down to write, a monstrous reader looms up who sits down beside me and continually mutters, "I don't get it, I don't see it, I don't want it. . . ." I know that I must never let him affect my vision, must never let him gain control over my thinking, must never listen to his demands unless they accord with my conscience; yet I feel I must make him see what I have to show, even if my means of making him see have to be extreme.[44]

While readers may find all of these instances of O'Connor's humor entertaining, we may also be left asking, "What's the point?" Was O'Connor simply a funny woman, or was there a greater purpose for her humor?

One does not have to be acquainted with O'Connor's work for long to realize that she rarely does anything simply for the sake of doing it. As Ralph Wood notes, "her comedy always has a moral bite."[45] At the same time, she is also not concerned with morality for the sake of morality. Her intent goes much deeper: not an examination of actions but an examination of the heart and its relationship to God. Some of the most humorous situations expose the prideful self-reliance of her characters. When we read of the theft of Hulga Hopewell's leg or Mary Grace hurling a book at Ruby Turpin, we chuckle inwardly. But much more than our entertainment is at work here. These characters are not actively searching for God's grace, yet the self-sufficiency upon which they have built their lives is shown to be shifting sand more than the rock they thought it was. As a result, they do find God's grace, or at least are made ready to receive it.

KEEPING THE FAITH

As previously mentioned, O'Connor's faith was the lifeblood of her work. In fact, she saw a great deal of irony in her ill reception by Catholic readers because she felt she wrote the way she did *because* she was a Catholic, not in spite of it. In fact, she claimed that if she were not Catholic, "I would have no reason to write, no reason to see, no reason ever to feel horrified or even to enjoy anything."[46] Some have called her simple-minded and berated her for her confidence in the Church, but

O'Connor's faith was simply part of who she was, not a framework upon which she could prop her plots, themes, symbols, and characters.

Because her religious beliefs were such an integral part of who she was, she could not keep from expressing them in her work. Therefore, it is important to examine exactly what her beliefs were. According to O'Connor, the central fact of human existence is this: "that [humanity] has for all its horror, been found by God to be worth dying for."[47] Evil and Satan are real entities, doing constant spiritual battle for the hearts of men and women who must choose between good and evil. This aspect of her work has persuaded many critics to place her within the Gothic school of literature, which involves, in very general terms, employing the supernatural to create a sense of mysteriousness and create characters who experience the terror of isolation from family, community, and/or God. While this classification of O'Connor's work is valid, her beliefs about God, evil, and Satan were an inextricable part of her identity as a Christian, not necessarily as a "Gothic writer." As resolute as she was in her beliefs, O'Connor nevertheless saw and accepted the faults of the Catholic Church and, from time to time, entertained doubts about her faith. In one of her most thorough explications of her faith, she responded to a letter from Alfred Corn, an Emory University student who heard O'Connor lecture on campus. After encountering so many conflicting ideas and religious systems during his first year at Emory, Corn was struggling with his own religious values, and O'Connor responded to his letter with warmth, wisdom, and empathy. She assured him that nurturing one's faith is a demanding task and that intellectual conflict is simply something a Christian deals with his or her entire life. She wrote to Corn that the mysteries of God and the conflicts between the beliefs of different world religions were troublesome to her at one point in her life; however, she was troubled by it no longer because she had learned "how incomprehensible God must necessarily be to be the God of heaven and earth."[48]

Despite her adherence to the Catholic Church, O'Connor's religious vision was not narrow. As Ralph Wood states, she was not interested in attracting an "'inside' audience who would need to know about rosaries and novenas, monasteries and abbeys, popes and encyclicals."[49] In fact, there are very few Catholic characters in her stories—a Catholic heroine in "A Temple of the Holy Ghost," priests and nuns in "The Enduring Chill," and a few others scattered here and there.

Instead of drawing on religious traditions more "native" to her, O'Connor largely drew from what she saw around her: evangelical Protestants. Despite the liturgical differences between this group and her own religious heritage, O'Connor saw the two as more alike than different because they share the same concern with humanity's need for grace. The differences between the two groups surface in their attitudes toward the sacraments. While O'Connor believed that people receive grace through faith in God but also through receiving sacraments, such as the Eucharist and baptism, the evangelical Protestants of her region believed that grace comes through faith alone. In addition, evangelical Protestants focused on bringing the unconverted to redemption in Christ, while O'Connor focused on those already converted who need a daily reminder that they must totally depend on God and the work of His grace in their lives. However, O'Connor was able to overlook these differences with her "cousins in Christ"[50] because she felt they were differences in attitude toward the role of the church, not toward the role of God in the lives of people. The fact that the two groups both believe that God desires to redeem fallen humanity but will only do so when individuals freely accept Him was enough to help O'Connor excuse any differences in doctrine or focus between Catholicism and Protestantism.

O'Connor also realized that she was one of a relative few in a secular society who still held to traditional Christian theology. Therefore, this Christian vision was not a particularly popular or easy one to communicate to her readers because of the decline of conventional religion and Biblical knowledge during her lifetime, even in the Bible Belt of the South. Regardless of any limitations she perceived in her readership, her faith remained the dominant pattern in the fabric of her life and work, and instead of seeing it as a limitation to her art, she saw it as the power that enabled her to depict the world as it truly is. She was first and foremost an artist, but she felt her adherence to the Church and its tenets would improve her work, not hinder it. As a result, she never apologized for who she was or what she wrote, no matter who was scandalized or offended.

THE WAY TO GRACE

O'Connor's work explores many issues that are common to literature of all types, but her works have a different twist, because the issues are examined through the lens of her faith in God and in the Catholic Church. First among her common themes was pride, which she felt was at the center of humanity's fall from God and need for God's grace. In O'Connor's view, most sins, whether it be murder, jealousy, or zealotry, boiled down to pride. Most of her stories follow a pattern: a character who is consumed with himself or herself, yet still hungers for a fulfillment that O'Connor felt only God could provide, encounters a turning point in which an epiphany is possible and grace is offered. The character typically has a choice to either accept the grace offered to him or her or reject it. As one reads more and more of O'Connor's work, this pattern soon becomes expected; however, the characters' reactions are hardly predictable as few of them respond in exactly the same fashion.

Three of the best illustrations of this pattern are in her stories "Good Country People," "The Lame Shall Enter First," and "Revelation." While the issues of pride and grace are examined in all three stories, the situations used to bring the characters to grace and the characters' responses to grace are all different. In "Good Country People," Joy/Hulga Hopewell is humiliated in a cruel but fairly harmless way, and while she is prepared to receive grace, her response is beyond the range of the story. Conversely, Sheppard in "The Lame Shall Enter First" must deal with tragedy and violence within his own family, and while he realizes his blame in the events that occur, the story ends without showing how these shocking events ultimately change (or fail to change) his life. In yet another twist on this theme, Ruby Turpin in "Revelation" is not only prepared for grace, but we see her humbled as she experiences a full epiphany and accepts the grace offered her.

"GOOD COUNTRY PEOPLE"

Joy Hopewell, the protagonist of "Good Country People" who has a philosophy PhD, a wooden leg, and a weak heart, has changed her name to the ugly-sounding name Hulga to reflect her bitter attitude toward life and her desire to be different from what her mother and others around her want her to be. While she does not want to be confined to her mother's mindless, superficial characterizations of what is "right" for people, Hulga is not a true dissenter. Instead, she simply wishes to conform to and find her identity in a different group. She resents being stuck with her mother on their farm and having to listen to her and her neighbor Mrs. Freeman exchange clichéd conversations. She wishes that she were far away "in a university lecturing to people who knew what she was talking about." Instead, she mopes around, purposefully wearing a yellow sweatshirt with a horse on it and a tattered old skirt to irritate her mother: "[Hulga] thought this was funny; Mrs. Hopewell thought it was idiotic and showed simply that she was still a child. She was brilliant but she didn't have a grain of sense." Much of her self-absorption seems to come in the form of her wooden leg, for she tries to make the prosthesis as noticeable as possible instead of doing the opposite, which one would expect her to do. She is described as joining Mrs. Hopewell and Mrs. Freeman at the breakfast table by making as much noise as possible: "she could walk without making the awful noise but she made it—Mrs. Hopewell was certain—because it was ugly-sounding."[51] As Sheldon Currie states, "Watching her graceless stomp, the maker of her leg would think himself a clumsy failure. Hulga is far from trying to incorporate her leg ... the leg becomes her center and she its satellite."[52]

Hulga's puffed up sense of self is revealed when she encounters Manley Pointer, a traveling Bible salesman whom she sees as an ignoramus because of his apparent religious beliefs; he is just the type of "good country people" her mother loves and she detests. At full height of her condescension, she plots to seduce Manley after he invites her on a picnic, imagining that she will open his eyes to a "deeper understanding of life." What happens instead is that Manley opens one of his Bibles to reveal that it is hollow and contains pornographic playing cards, alcohol, and condoms—evidence of who he really is. Furthermore, he convinces a bewildered Hulga to let him into an intimate part of herself by showing him where her artificial leg attaches. Stunned by the revelation of the real Manley, Hulga falls into the language she has heard from the mother she has always wanted to be the most unlike: "Aren't you ... aren't you just good country people?" Manley later responds both to her protests and her smug pronunciation that she does not believe in anything, including God, with, "You ain't so smart. I've been believing in nothing ever since I was born!"[53] Manley steals Hulga's leg and leaves her stranded in the barn. With Hulga's pride pierced, O'Connor leaves the reader thinking of the very types of clichés Mrs. Freeman and Mrs. Hopewell have uttered throughout the story as Manley "pulls her leg" and leaves Hulga "without a leg to stand on." As Frederick Asals states, "If Manley Pointer turns out to be as hollow as the Bible he reveals in the barn, so Hulga is as empty as the wooden leg it was based on."[54]

While the phallic name Manley Pointer and the nearly incessant exchange of clichés provide a great deal of humor in the story, Hulga's loss of her leg may be the ultimate humorous event, especially because of the clichés it invokes. However, Clinton Trowbridge claims that what may be the most humorous event may also be the most important in that it prepares Hulga for her moment of grace by making her vulnerable: "Thrown off balance, she has already been forced to rely on someone else, and this experience, this first surrender of herself, has in it the quality of what must be her ultimate surrender to Christ."[55] The fact that Hulga has resisted surrender her entire life in her struggle against her mother, who seems determined to make Hulga into an image of herself, makes it that much more difficult for Hulga to throw off her own pride, necessitating drastic action to prepare her for the moment of grace. In addition to losing her leg, Hulga also misplaces her glasses while in the loft with Manley, "but her internal vision is readjusted."[56] While the story ends before we know of Hulga's response beyond being abandoned by Manley in the barn, we do know that she is at least prepared for her moment of grace, whether she accepts it or not.

"THE LAME SHALL ENTER FIRST"

In a very different set of circumstances, we read a similar story of pride that leads to a great fall in the life of Sheppard, a city recreation director in "The Lame Shall Enter First," who is raising his 10-year-old son, Norton, after the death of his wife. Feeling that his efforts toward raising Norton are wasted, he takes a special interest in 14-year-old Rufus Johnson, a juvenile delinquent with a deformed foot, whom he comes to know through his work as a counselor at the reformatory where Rufus has been incarcerated. Sheppard sees Rufus's intelligence as greater than Norton's, making Rufus a more deserving recipient of the "wisdom" Sheppard intends to impart to him as he attempts to create a son in his own image. Rufus, knowing that he can use Sheppard's interest in him to his own advantage, breaks into Sheppard's home and then is invited by Sheppard to live with him and Norton. Rufus claims to be under Satan's control, and while his actions may be reprehensible throughout the story, he recognizes Sheppard's inflated view of himself and his ability to "redeem" Rufus. He says to Norton, "God, kid . . . how do you stand it? . . . He thinks he's Jesus Christ!"[57] Ironically, Sheppard reprimands Norton for not being sensitive to Rufus's "suffering," while Sheppard himself is not sensitive to the suffering of his son, who continues to grieve for his mother who has been dead over a year. Because of his intense, lasting grief, Norton takes Rufus's descriptions of heaven and hell literally, prompting his father to insist that Norton's mother is neither in heaven nor hell but has simply ceased to exist. He refuses to "lower himself" to what he considers an easy, religious explanation: that his dead wife is in heaven where he and Norton will eventually be reunited with her. Norton, who does not want to believe that his mother no longer exists anywhere in the universe, instead believes Rufus's assertion that she is "on high" among the stars, and he can only get to her by being dead himself.

Sheppard continues his efforts to reform Rufus, offering to buy him a pair of custom-made shoes that will correct the limp he has from the deformed foot, but all of his efforts to reach out to Rufus are in vain. He fails to realize that Rufus does not want to be made into his image and prefers to remain crippled rather than become like Sheppard. Likewise,

Norton feels abandoned by him, especially after he hears Sheppard call Rufus "son" and after Sheppard refuses to come to him when Norton calls to him from his bed. When Rufus is later arrested, Sheppard tries to defend his actions by telling a reporter, "I did everything I knew how for him. I did more for him than I did for my own child." Moments later, he realizes the truth of his own statement and his true motives for helping Rufus: "He had stuffed his own emptiness with good works like a glutton. He had ignored his own child to feed his vision of himself."[58] As Paulson notes, "The terrible gap between Sheppard's limited, this-worldly short-sightedness and the religious perspective is evident in the dramatic irony here—the gap between Sheppard's pretense to goodness and his failure to extend charity to his own son."[59] But Sheppard appears to have realized his moment of grace too late, for even as he vows to do better by Norton, he finds Norton in the attic where he had been looking at the stars, longing for his mother, and is now hanging from a rafter because he felt no love from his father. Norton has taken his own life to reach his dead mother who loved him. "No summary can do justice to the persuasiveness of this story which says unmistakably that Christian believer, no matter how sinful, is infinitely to be preferred to a do-gooder atheist."[60]

Robert Coles recalls a remark made by a psychiatry intern in a discussion group after O'Connor's death: "Flannery O'Connor spots the phony everywhere, but she doesn't call it a name, she puts it into a story."[61] Both Hulga and Sheppard are revealed for the counterfeits they are. However, while Hulga loses her leg, Sheppard loses much, much more, and both characters help issue O'Connor's indictment of modern society: "If the liberal, atheistic, man-centered society of modern times is dedicated to manipulating others in order to 'save' them, to transform them into flattering images of their own egos, then there is no love involved. . . . This kind of love is deadly, because it believes itself to be selfless."[62] Exposing such phoniness is a matter of course for O'Connor, for the counterfeit can never be made genuine without submission to the grace of Christ. Again, while we as readers do not always know if characters receive the grace offered to them, we always see them at least spiritually sifted and prepared within to receive it.

"REVELATION"

In one of O'Connor's final stories, "Revelation," we get a much more lighthearted look at this need for grace, and unlike "Good Country People" and "The Lame Shall Enter First," we get a greater glimpse into a character's response to the offering of grace. The main character in "Revelation,"

Ruby Turpin, is a farmwoman who does all the right things. She is a good-natured woman who pokes fun at her own rotundity and makes friendly conversation to pass the time in a crowded doctor's waiting room as she tends to her husband Claud's ulcerous leg. She appears to be a model of Christian charity—a devoted wife, a generous member of the community, a dedicated church-goer. Yet like so many other of O'Connor's protagonists, she's a fake. We as readers are privy to her thoughts as she scorns a "white trash" child with a runny nose and wishes she could run the doctor's office so that it would be run the "right" way. When one of the "white trash" women remarks that she got some jewelry by saving green stamps, Ruby secretly and caustically thinks, "Ought to have got you a wash rag and some soap." In fact, nearly every comment Ruby makes that is addressed to the "pleasant woman" (who is clearly upper class) about the "right" way to live—a way that the "pleasant woman" agrees with, of course—is followed by a silent thought addressed toward the "white trash." For example, when Ruby says to the "pleasant woman," "When you got something … you got to look after it," she immediately thinks to herself regarding the "white trash," "And when you ain't got a thing but breath and britches … you can afford to come to town every morning and just sit on the Court House coping and spit."[63]

While Ruby never speaks as bluntly and as harshly as she thinks, some of her genuine opinions do seep out as she very obviously excludes from conversation everyone but the "pleasant woman" and openly states her view that blacks are lazy and uppity. It is these very opinions that spark the hateful contempt of Mary Grace, the daughter accompanying the "pleasant woman." Mary Grace makes no attempt to hide her disdain for Ruby as she slams her *Human Development* book closed, white-knuckles it, and stares at Ruby with hatred.

Of all of O'Connor's protagonists, Ruby Turpin is perhaps the most childish. She has a certain view of the way the world should be, and she clings to it with an infantile stubbornness. Ruby even tries to find some sort of comfort in the scheme she sees in the world by reflecting on it as she drifts off to sleep, almost as if she hopes to bring sweet dreams into her mind by thinking happy thoughts just before bed. She ponders an imaginary conversation with Jesus in which He asks her if she would rather be black or be white trash. In a sadly humorous way, she begs, "'Please, Jesus, please … just let me wait until there's another place available,'" but alas, she must choose. So she settles on being black: "'All right, make me a nigger then—but that don't mean a trashy one.' And he would have made her a neat clean respectable Negro woman, herself but black." At other times, she thinks on the social hierarchy she has created in her mind: trashy blacks at the bottom, white trash just above them, home owners next, then home and land owners (the category where she and Claud fit), and then people with a lot of money and land and big houses at the top. At this point, her hierarchy seems to break down as she must account for people whose families come from money but who lost their money, blacks who own houses and land, and people with money who are not as respectable as she and Claud. "Usually by the time she had fallen asleep all the classes of people were moiling and roiling around in her head, and she would dream they were all crammed together in a box car, being ridden off to be put in a gas oven." Ruby Turpin has a scheme of how the world *should* operate (because *she* says that's how it should be done), and when that scheme breaks down, even her imagination seems to reflect her preference for utter destruction over a life lived in any way other than the one she desires. Ultimately, however, she is satisfied with her life, even if the structure of the rest of the world does not fit her ideal, and at her most puffed up, "Her heart rose. [Jesus] had not made her a nigger or white-trash or ugly! He had made her herself and given her a little of everything. Jesus, thank you! she said. Thank you thank you thank you!"[64]

Just after Ruby experiences a similar fit of gratitude several paragraphs later, "the book struck her directly over her left eye." Mary Grace has had all she can take of the self-righteous Ruby Turpin, and she hurls her *Human Development* book at her, begins yelling, goes for Ruby's throat, and finally says, "Go back to hell when you came from, you old wart hog."[65] The brawl is broken up, and Mary Grace is taken away, presumably for some kind of psychiatric care, but Ruby is now a different woman.

After she and Claud make their way home and she recovers from the shock of the physical attack, she must deal with the most painful blow: Mary Grace's indictment of her as a wart hog from hell. In tears, Ruby vehemently tries to convince herself that she is *not* like the "white trash" woman in the waiting room to whom the label "wart hog from hell" could be more accurately applied; despite her passionate appeals, she is not convinced. Much like Sheppard, she is hit full in the face with the reality of her own puffed up smugness, and at that point, she is no longer hurt but is angry. Her anger burns so strongly that neither a kiss from Claud nor a cup of cold water for their black field hands will assuage it. In fact, her anger only grows hotter and fiercer, making her "look like [she] might have swallowed a mad dog."[66] Certainly, anger toward Mary Grace would be justified, but we quickly learn as Ruby cleans the pigs in their "pig parlor" that she is not as angry with Mary Grace as she is with God Himself. In a quiet fury, she asks, "What do you send me a message like that for? ... How am I a hog and me both? How am I saved and from hell too? ... Why me?" While she is spiritually alert enough to recognize that she has indeed received a message from God, she has still missed the point, for she begins to disparage the very same groups—blacks and white trash—that she had been mentally and verbally denigrating before Mary Grace attacked her, saying that she could still act like white trash ("Dip snuff and spit in every puddle and have it all over my face.") or like a "nigger" ("Lay down in the middle of the road and stop traffic. Roll on the ground.") if God likes trash better than he likes "good" people like her. At the zenith of her rage, she shouts, "Who do you think you are?"[67] Finally, she receives a response from God, but it is not the one she expects. Instead of being told that she is right, it is, according to Ralph Wood, as if God responds by asking, "Who do you think *you* are?"[68] He opens the heavens to reveal to Ruby the *true* hierarchy of the world—not as she wishes it to be but as it truly is: a whole band of people she would have labeled "white trash" or "niggers" or lunatics or freaks in a jubilant parade toward heaven, with people like her and Claud bringing up the rear while "even their virtues were being burned away."[69] As Wood notes, those Ruby labels as "white trash" and "niggers" may, for all their faults, be God's favorites because the "respectable" people like the Turpins are often "spiritually arrogant," a fault more destructive than most other sin.[70] The story leaves no doubt that Ruby Turpin is a recipient of God's grace by faith alone, not through her good works, a fact of which she is made painfully aware, not by a prank or an horrific death but by an angry college girl bold enough to throw a book at her. It is just this kind of acceptance of grace on which Maurice Lévy comments: "In these special moments in which the characters' experience is made pure and universal, there is no place for either the ironic or the grotesque, and God Himself seems to live again. Not the triumphant, security-giving God that societies need and constantly restore for their own particular ends, but He who is an open wound."[71]

IDENTITY AND SELF-KNOWLEDGE

In several instances in O'Connor's work, it is not pride that brings a character to grace but a quest for self-knowledge. One of these stories is "Parker's Back," which O'Connor wrote as she was literally dying, and which is one of a handful of stories that does not end in a death of some sort. In this story, we meet Parker and his wife, Sarah Ruth. The two meet when Parker's truck breaks down near her family's home. Parker feels he is being watched and fakes hurting his hand so that he can curse loudly and draw attention to himself. Sure enough, his first acquaintance with

Sarah Ruth is when she storms out to his truck, slaps him, and reprimands him for cursing. It is at this point that we learn of Parker's obsession: his tattoos. He has tattoos on nearly every part of his body and got them in all parts of the world after seeing a tattooed man at the fair when he was 14. Seeing this man is a turning point for Parker: "Until he saw the man at the fair, it did not enter his head that there was anything out of the ordinary about the fact that he existed ... a peculiar unease settled in him."[72] He sees unity in the designs on this man's body and begins his quest for this kind of wholeness. As Vigen Guroian mentions, "His search for God was begun, although he did not call it that. And Parker had discovered the mystery of his own being as a creature of God made in God's own image."[73]

Shortly after Parker begins getting tattoos, drinking, and carousing, his mother, lamenting what her son is becoming, drags him to a revival service. When Parker realizes where his mother is taking him, he runs away, lies about his age, and joins the Navy. These events are described in flashback, but Parker's crisis is clear from the second paragraph as he describes Sarah Ruth's attitude toward life:

> Sometimes he supposed that she mad married him because she meant to save him. At other times he had a suspicion that she actually liked everything she said she didn't. He could account for her one way or another; it was himself he could not understand.[74]

Caught in the middle of the age old body/spirit conflict, he will not even acknowledge his real, Biblical name, Obadiah Elihue. After joining the Navy, Parker gets one tattoo after another, seemingly with the hope that each one will fill the emptiness inside him. It is almost as if he thinks he can save himself. In fact, later in the story, Parker comments to a tattoo artist, "I ain't got no use for [religion]. A man can't save his self from whatever it is he don't deserve none of my sympathy." Even as he speaks, Parker seems to know his words are not true, that he cannot save himself: they "leave his mouth like wraiths and ... evaporate at once as if he had never uttered them."[75] Each time he gets a tattoo, he is satisfied with it for a month or so and then the newness wears off, prompting him to get another one. He also refuses to get tattoos on his back because he wants to be able to see them. Clearly, Parker's identity is tied up in his tattoos.

Dan Curley has noted that "... the louder a character proclaims his rebellion against God, the stronger is his desire to believe in God."[76] Parker certainly seems to fit this mold, and he is drawn to Sarah Ruth, the daughter of a traveling evangelist, because, with all her talk of vanity and sin, she knows who she is: she is God's child and His representative on earth—at least in her own mind. When they first meet, she insults his tattoos repeatedly, even referring to his eagle tattoo as a chicken, yet when she goes back into her house, he cannot bring himself to leave. In fact, he returns with a bushel of apples the next day, claiming that he is not going to be "outdone" by the likes of her. He is rudely treated by both Sarah Ruth and her mother this time, and although he promises to return the next day with a bushel of peaches, he has no intention of doing so. Yet he finds himself there anyway, bringing a bushel of peaches. This pattern continues, and the two eventually marry, even though Parker swears he wants nothing to do with her. It seems that even though Sarah Ruth constantly nags him about how God will judge him if he doesn't change his ways, Parker is attracted to her self-assuredness: she knows who she is in a way that he does not. Just as he swore to never return to her before they ever married, he swears he will leave her, but he returns every night, as if he cannot help himself, even though he is miserable. He considers getting a tattoo to comfort himself, but the only space left on his body for a tattoo is his back.

Finally, Parker is so unhappy that he *must* get a tattoo. One day when he is out working on the tractor, he is pondering a design for the tattoo on his back, runs the tractor into the only tree in the field, and is thrown from the tractor. In a scene reminiscent of God speaking to Moses through the burning bush, the tree bursts into flames, and Parker shouts, "GOD ABOVE!"[77] Just as Moses is commanded to remove his shoes because he is standing on holy ground, Parker loses his shoes, one to the flames and one under the tractor. Parker runs from this encounter with God and goes straight to the city to get a tattoo, again to assuage the emptiness within that only God can fill. Even as he runs, he knows he has reached a turning point in his life: "He only knew that there had been a great change in his life, a leap forward into a worse unknown, and that there was nothing he could do about it. It was for all intents accomplished." In the hopes of winning over Sarah Ruth, he had previously decided his next tattoo would be religious in nature, and he receives what he thinks is a direct word from God to choose a tattoo of a Byzantine Christ. The tattoo artist begins the tattoo but cannot finish it in one day, so Parker goes to the Haven of Light Christian Mission to spend the night. While there, he decides he must be losing his mind since he longs for Sarah Ruth, specifically thinking of her eyes, which "appeared soft and dilatory compared with the eyes [of the Byzantine Christ] in the book ... he could still feel their penetration. He felt as though, under their gaze, he was as transparent as the wing of a fly." Parker sits in an alley after getting the tattoo, and although he has not had the kind of salvation experience that Sarah Ruth would find valid, it seems he realizes that he is now Christ's: "The eyes that were now forever on his back were eyes to be obeyed. He was as certain of it as he had ever been of anything."[78]

After visiting a bar and running into some old friends, Parker returns home with his fresh tattoo, convinced that Sarah Ruth will finally be truly endeared to him because of the Byzantine Christ on his back. Ironically, she doesn't even recognize the face on his back as that of Christ, she calls him an idolater, and she proceeds to drive him from the house by beating him on the back with a broom, leaving the Byzantine Christ with red welts all over his face. Parker goes out to a pecan tree in the yard and weeps.

While the story leaves us hanging as to the fate of Obadiah Elihue Parker, it is clear that he has not only tried to reach out to Sarah Ruth but also to God. Ironically, even though Sarah Ruth's Christianity is not very appealing, she is instrumental in forcing Parker to look beyond his attempt to save himself. In fact, it is she who forces him to speak aloud his Biblical name, Obadiah Elihue. Obadiah means "servant of God," and Elihue means "God is he," and when Parker is made to speak this name audibly after he gets the tattoo of Christ, he experiences a spiritual awakening as he accepts who he really is, "the light pouring through him, turning his spider web soul into a perfect arabesque of colors, a garden of trees and birds and beasts."[79] As John Desmond asserts, Sarah Ruth "effects symbolically the transformation of the whole person by insisting that Parker use his own biblical name. Thus when she subdues him with a broom until welts appear on the Byzantine tattoo, she is chastising his errant spirit to return him to who he truly is."[80] Because the conclusion of the story is so open-ended, we can only speculate about Parker's future; however, he is clearly a broken man, one who is ready to receive God's grace.

Just like Parker, Hazel Motes, the main character of O'Connor's novel *Wise Blood,* claims that he does not need salvation from God because he can save himself. As a result, Haze goes on a journey similar to Parker's—a quest for self-knowledge—but with much less positive results. He is determined to not become a religious fanatic like his grandfather, "a waspish old man who had ridden over three counties with Jesus hidden in his head like a stinger" and who would drive around to different communities, preaching while standing on top of his car. At the same time, he has an identity handed to him and knows from age 12 that he is going to become a preacher. He carries his Bible and his mother's glasses with him when he joins the Army, and he is convinced that he can remain sinless and avoid his calling: "There was already a deep black wordless

conviction in him that the way to avoid Jesus was to avoid sin."[81] When
the novel opens with Haze on a train, the reader wonders, is he truly
a hardened World War II veteran who believes that religion is for crack-
pots? Or is he a confused young man who is longing to fill an emptiness
inside that only God can fill?

We know from an event of his youth that he does have an awareness
of sin. When his father takes him to a carnival, he connives his way into
a display advertised as "SINsational" and "EXclusive," even though he
knows his highly religious mother would disapprove of his being there.
When he gets home, his mother immediately knows he has seen something
sinful and hits him across the legs with a stick, saying "Jesus died to redeem
you." Haze responds by saying, "I never ast him"[82] and goes out on his own
the next day to do penance for his sin by filling his shoes with rocks and
walking over a mile while wearing them, thinking that this act will satisfy
Jesus and remove Haze's need for him. Yet, he senses that it does not.

Obviously, Haze rebels against this calling to ministry nearly from the
moment he senses it. At the same time, the adult Haze seems to have
some awareness of his heritage and even pride in it as he repeatedly tells
the porter on the train that he is from Eastrod, expecting some sort of
response of admiration. On the other hand, he also speaks with pride
to Mrs. Wally Hitchcock that he is going to Taulkinham, where he has
never been and knows no one but where he is "going to do some things
[he] never [has] done before." It is at this point that he also begins to
antagonize Mrs. Wally Hitchcock about being "redeemed," even though
everything she has said up to this point has been meaningless small talk
with no religious component whatsoever. He is further frustrated in the
taxi he takes to Leora Watts's house when the taxi driver assumes he is
a preacher because of the suit and hat he is wearing. The cabbie says, "It
ain't only the hat ... It's a look in your face somewheres," to which Haze
replies, "Listen ... get this: I don't believe in anything."[83]

Despite his claim, he is inexplicably drawn to the blind street
preacher, Asa Hawks, and his daughter, Sabbath Lily. He follows them
to a theater where they are planning to distribute tracts to the audience members as they leave, and even though they ask him to help
distribute their tracts, he begins telling people as they leave the theater
that they are just as good as anyone else and don't need Jesus. Hence,
the Church Without Christ is spontaneously formed, with Haze as its
preacher and Enoch Emery as his disciple—a church "where the blind
don't see and the lame don't walk and what's dead stays that way."[84]
He buys a car and begins his street ministry, preaching from it just as
his grandfather did.

In his mind, anyone who preaches Christ, like Asa Hawks, is his enemy, so he decides to seduce Sabbath Lily as a way to discredit Asa and Christianity as a whole. It does not take him long, however, to learn that Hawks is not really blind. He had only promised to blind himself as an act of faith but lost his nerve at the last minute. To Haze, this proves once again that the gospel is not genuine but is as fake as Asa Hawks's blindness. When Hoover Shoats (also known as Onnie Jay Holy), another counterfeit street preacher, tries to take over Haze's territory with the Church of Christ Without Christ as a money-making scheme, Haze kills Solace Layfield, Shoats's disciple. He then vows to do what Asa Hawks could not: blind himself with lime. He also puts gravel and bits of broken glass in his socks, recalling his earlier act of penance, and wears barbed wire wrapped around his chest. He begins a relationship with Mrs. Flood, his landlady, but one day, he leaves, wearing his suit and hat, and is later found by the police in a drainage ditch and dies shortly thereafter.

Clearly, Haze's ideas about Jesus begin in rebellion but end in submission. As Frederick Hoffman states, "Motes fights the idea and the image of Christ ... But he is so earnest, so frantic and stubborn about it, that it is obvious to anyone that he is obsessed by the challenge of Christ and will one day surrender to it."[85] Indeed, he does surrender to it, and instead of finding an identity independent of Christ, he seems to find an identity because of Christ.

At the same time, he destroys himself, first by blinding himself, a symbolic action which shows he is moving toward greater insight. As Laura B. Kennelly points out, Haze trusts in literal vision throughout the novel, first by carrying around and using his mother's glasses, even though the prescription is not appropriate for him. He trusts in what he can see, but he makes many errors of vision in the early parts of the novel, such as mistaking the porter on the train, who is from Chicago, for a black man he knew from Parrum, a town close to Eastrod.[86] Ironically, much like Oedipus, Haze runs from the truth for a long time, and when he realizes it, he blinds himself and later wanders out in the cold and exposes himself to the elements. "Motes changes his course, from a defiant anti-preacher to a dedicated penitent, on the strength of a discovery that Asa Hawks had faked blindness, and did not have the courage to go through with the act of blinding himself, to prove that Jesus had redeemed him. Motes substitutes a real blinding, and becomes, abruptly, the young penitent, the self-appointed saint."[87] All of this is necessary to reveal to Haze who he really is: a sinner in need of God's grace. As Deborah Moddelmog states, again making a connection between Haze and Oedipus, "Oedipus' history reveals the futility of attempting to evade a fate marked out by a higher power, of denying the truth about oneself, and of relying on one's senses to apprehend reality. These were exactly the points O'Connor was trying to make from a Christian perspective in *Wise Blood*."[88]

GROTESQUE

Despite characters such as Parker and Hazel Motes, O'Connor's primary means of illustrating the need for grace is creating characters such as Hulga and Sheppard who are exceptionally arrogant and self-righteous. One of her primary means of illustrating this kind of pride is her use of the grotesque; in fact, Patricia Yaeger asserts that O'Connor "uses the greatest proportion of grotesque personae per paragraph of any southern writer."[89] The grotesque is typically defined as writing that involves characters that are bizarre, absurd, unattractive, abnormal, distorted, deformed, and often repulsive, either in outer physical appearance, inner spiritual condition, or both. Her view of humans as naturally depraved and desperately in need of God's grace departed sharply from the Agrarians, a group of writers and literary critics who believed in humanity's natural goodness. O'Connor did not employ the grotesque as simply a literary technique. Instead, she used it to demonstrate humanity's separation from God—the one whose grace can restore that broken fellowship.

As far as situations and events are concerned in the grotesque, "contradiction is its fundamental principle. It offers no resolutions. It lacks the picture-perfect happy ending of comedy or the moral judgment of satire; and it completely derides the transcendental closure of tragedy."[90] Many believe that O'Connor's background as a cartoonist contributed to her tendency to employ such incongruous, often disquieting images and characters. According to O'Connor, the term was often applied to Southern authors in a derogatory manner simply because Southern writing is often misunderstood by those outside Southern society. Furthermore, she stated that the South's religious roots make it easier for Southerners to recognize, use, and understand grotesque situations and characters: "Whenever I am asked why Southern writers particularly have a penchant for writing about freaks, I say it is because we are still able to recognize one. To be able to recognize a freak, you have to have some conception of the whole man, and in the South the general conception of man is still, in the main, theological."[91]

She maintained that Christians are also able to identify the grotesque, and the challenge for a writer such as herself is to help her readers see what is grotesque when they are accustomed to viewing what is actually grotesque as normal. As she stated in many of her essays, lectures, and interviews, it was this lack of a theological base in her readership that prompted her to employ the grotesque, knowing that the violent, abnormal, and absurd characters and situations she would employ would shock her readers and get their attention: "to the hard of hearing you shout, and for the almost-blind you draw large and startling figures."[92] Many agree that part of the reason we as readers fail to recognize the grotesque when we see it is that we are too much like the grotesque characters she portrays. J. M. G. Le Clézio states, "If the world that Flannery O'Connor has created shocks us, it is not so much because it is confused and brutal, but because it is true."[93] O'Connor is clever in her creation of characters such as Sheppard, Hulga, or Ruby Turpin in whom we can immediately see the kind of self-importance we despise and at whom we laugh derisively, only in the end to make us see that, in some way, we are just like them. At one time or another, haven't we all ignored those who needed us most in order to fulfill our own desires and fill our own internal emptiness? Haven't we all looked with disdain at those "simpler" than we are? Haven't we all defined our identities in terms of social class, race, and religion? O'Connor thought so, and she felt many readers were not receptive to seeing themselves in her stories, stating, "I find that nothing irritates the average reader so much as fiction which he considers grotesque. When he reads it, he appears to look at himself in a distorting mirror, and his natural reaction is to scream, 'This is a lie!'"[94] Some, however, have apparently found themselves in this "distorting mirror," for as Fred Chappell so honestly states, "It's not that I am dismayed or baffled by her characters. Indeed, I find them all too familiar."[95]

Others believe that O'Connor's affinity and sympathy for those with deformities led her to utilize the grotesque in her work. Although she was not permanently deformed in any physical way because of the lupus, the side effects she experienced, plus her lifelong reliance on crutches, must have given her a window into the world of those who are different from the norm. She even seemed to have an affinity for the deformed and the abnormal in the birds she kept as pets. In just one instance, O'Connor wanted a pair of swans but found them to be too expensive. When friend De Vene Harold found a cheap pair of mated swans for her, O'Connor was thrilled to learn one swan had a strange growth on its body, the other was blind in one eye, and the two hated each other. She took a great deal of pride in her birds and even sent Harold pictures of them. Likewise, many of her characters are physically deformed: for example, Hulga has a wooden leg; Tom Shiftlet is missing part of his arm; and Rufus Johnson has a deformed foot. Even if O'Connor could not control the effects of lupus on her own body, she could control the bodies of her characters, according to Katherine Hemple Prown. However, most of these characters also possess a more troubling spiritual deformity, usually pride, and perhaps the most deceptive characters are those who have no physical deformity but only a spiritual one, such as Sheppard, Ruby Turpin, Sarah Ruth, Julian, the Misfit, and the Grandmother. At the same time, these characters who are the most deformed spiritually (whether they are deformed physically or not) are the ones who have the greatest potential to receive grace.

O'Connor came face to face with the grotesque in real life when an order of Dominican nuns who operated the Our Lady of Perpetual Help Free Cancer Home in Atlanta asked her to write either a fictional or factual account of the life of Mary Ann, a girl afflicted with a tumor on one side of her face. Mary Ann came to the Home to live when she was three and was expected to live only six more months; instead, she lived to be 12 years old and was such a source of inspiration for the nuns and others that the nuns wanted to commemorate her life in some way, hence the book O'Connor was asked to write. Not being one to romanticize children and getting the impression that the nuns wanted her to do just that (even though they claimed they "did not want a pious little recital"),[96] O'Connor declined the offer to write the book but did encourage the nuns to write it themselves and even offered to help them with editing and preparing the manuscript for publication.

After looking at Mary Ann's picture, something held O'Connor's attention. She did not romanticize Mary Ann's appearance, claiming that it was "plainly grotesque." Yet something about her captivated O'Connor. She never expected the nuns to write a book about Mary Ann, but they did. And when O'Connor received it, she grimaced, for it was full of things that "make the professional writer groan." Stylistically, it was vague and undramatic, yet she was captivated by the text as well. According to O'Connor, the nuns were able to capture the "mystery" of Mary Ann's life—of how a child could come into such a wretched condition and yet be so rich. O'Connor's answer? "She fell into the hands of women who are shocked at nothing and who love life so much that they spend their own lives making comfortable those who have been pronounced incurable of cancer." In addition, O'Connor seemed to make a logical yet often overlooked correlation between how we respond to the ill and how we respond to anyone who is underprivileged. O'Connor saw the capability to confront suffering directly and not look away from it as an essential part of Christian charity and even made a correlation between racism and repugnance toward the suffering when she wrote, "When tenderness is detached from the source of tenderness [Christ], its logical outcome is terror. It ends in forced labor camps an in the fumes of the gas chamber."[97]

Perhaps most important is the impact this literal encounter with gro-
tesqueness had on O'Connor's view of her own use of the grotesque. When
one of the nuns quizzed her on "why the grotesque (of all things) was [her]
vocation," another nun answered the inquiring nun quite astutely on
O'Connor's behalf: "It's your vocation too." Indeed, O'Connor seemed to
realize that the grotesque is not all about evil; most of us have enough evil
within us and see it all around us that we no longer even perceive it as
grotesque. Good, however, is another matter. As O'Connor stated, "... its
face too is grotesque ... in us the good is something under construction.
The modes of evil usually receive worthy expression. The modes of good
have to be satisfied with a cliché or a smoothing down that will soften
their real look. When we look into the face of good, we are liable to see a
face like Mary Ann's, full of promise."[98] While it is easy to focus on the evil
or even simply unattractive nature of O'Connor's grotesques, she seemed
to see the potential for good in them, if they would only surrender to the
kind of love that the nuns offered to Mary Ann: the unconditional, saving
love and grace of Christ on the cross. As a result of her view of Mary Ann's
life, her lifelong attraction to odd birds, and her own debilitating illness,
one might expect O'Connor's treatment of the grotesque to be more
sympathetic than it is. However, one must always remember O'Connor's
purposes: "Flannery O'Connor ... wielded a literary hatchet rather than
a handkerchief; she realized that only a stern intellect, an adamant faith,
and an accretion of humor which usually shaded into the grotesque could
confront suffering, violence, and evil in this world."[99]

How then does one confront suffering, violence, and evil in this world?
Through the workings of God's grace, a theme in O'Connor's work
that goes hand in hand with the theme of pride. In O'Connor's stories,
moments of grace are typically brought about by an unlikely force that
may be "outfitted as one of the devil's disciples rather than an angelic
presence,"[100] as in the revelation of Manley Pointer's true nature or the
suicide of Norton. While many have interpreted the wry tone of her letters and other writings as pessimistic, O'Connor clearly has hope for the
spiritual state of humanity and keeps a door into grace perpetually open
for characters in her story who most desperately need it. Critic Anne
Elizabeth Carson notes the recurring image of the tornado in O'Connor's
stories as an event "whirls into a character's life, heralding disaster and
calamity; most importantly, it almost always signals a portentous reckon-
ing."[101] In particular, she cites Rayber in *The Violent Bear It Away*, who
sees a tornado in a dream and is offered an opportunity for redemption,
and Ruby Turpin, whose encounter with Mary Grace in the doctor's office
is couched in terms of a tornado. Carson notes that the difference between

these two particular characters is that O'Connor seems to see little chance that Rayber will truly repent and live as a new creation, while hope for Ruby Turpin is intimated at the end of the story. Characters of physical and spiritual deformity alike "have access to revelation because God can come to them ... in his power and his terror and his glory. He comes to them not because they are good (that would be the sentimentality our weakened religious sensibility would wish for) but because he is real."[102]

VIOLENCE

Often, O'Connor's characters undergo redemption through violent means, an aspect of her work, like her use of the grotesque, that her readers often found shocking and, at times, even repulsive. The violence might not be so shocking except that her stories are inundated with it; nearly half end not just with death but with a surprising, especially brutal death, such as the suicide of Norton in "The Lame Shall Enter First" or the murder of an entire family in "A Good Man is Hard to Find." Several other writers whose work O'Connor read, including Edgar Allan Poe, Franz Kafka, and Fyodor Dostoyevsky, also included bizarre violence in their work.

Regardless of whether this violence makes O'Connor's work eccentric or not, critics have had to deal with it and have arrived at numerous explanations for the violence that some have deemed excessive in the stories of a "nice girl" from an upstanding Georgia family. Some argue that, while all of O'Connor's violence is not gratuitous, much of it must reflect a sinister side of her temperament which she could safely express through her art. Others have claimed that it must be an outlet for her anger at her physical condition, and Robin Darling Young has written that O'Connor was "a violent woman. Sitting quietly in front of a typewriter in faraway Milledgeville, Georgia, supplied with the eyesight of a bird of prey, Flannery O'Connor used ... insight and poetic expression, to force her characters right up to the edge of the artistic abyss. ... she was delighted to apply alcohol and the knife where her contemporaries' sickness was most malignant."[103] Granville Hicks claims that such violence is unavoidable because of the depth of evil depicted in her stories,[104] and Margaret Whitt blames the violence on the pretense of Southern manners that applies to external behavior only and eventually finds an explosive, often brutal outlet after it is repressed for so long.[105] Frederick Hoffman claims that her characters' resistance to the redemptive act often intensifies this violence.[106] According to Prown, O'Connor imbued her work with violence, especially against women, to distinguish her work from that of the typical Southern "lady" and to "display her allegiance to the disembodied male intellect."[107] O'Connor herself always insisted that violence was one of her tools to get her characters' and her readers' attention, as mentioned earlier. Ralph Wood holds to that same explanation, stating that "death is central to O'Connor's fiction because she regarded it as the terminus that compels us to fix the shape of our souls—whether we shall keep our lives for our own vain use, or whether we shall give them back in gratitude to God."[108]

While some sort of violent act exists in nearly every O'Connor story, a few are fairly innocuous to the reader while still giving the characters a rude awakening, such as when Mr. Head denies knowing his grandson Nelson in "The Artificial Nigger" or when Mary Grace throws the book at Ruby Turpin. In fact, Mary Grace's admonishment to Ruby to "Go back to hell where you came from, you old wart hog!"[109] is just as or even more startling than the act of hitting her in the head with the book, especially in light of the code of Southern etiquette, which never would have condoned such disrespectful talk among "ladies," especially from a younger woman toward an older one. Most violent events, however, are truly shocking, as O'Connor intended them to be, such as when grandfather and granddaughter beat each other to death in "A View of the Woods" or when a bull gores Mrs. May in "Greenleaf."

A GOOD MAN IS (INDEED) HARD TO FIND

Perhaps the work discussed most for its combination of violence and spiritual content is "A Good Man is Hard to Find." The grandmother in the story is a self-righteous manipulator who bosses her son around as if he is a child and commands no respect from her two grandchildren. Her materialistic, superficial priorities are evident as she is nearly obsessed with dressing well and as she recalls Mr. Teagarden, a former love interest who was a "good man" because he was rich and handsome. Even though Red Sammy Butts is described as fat, with his stomach "[hanging] over [his pants] like a sack of meal swaying under his shirt,"[110] and somewhat unattractive with his red face, the grandmother decides he too is a "good man," presumably because he is an entrepreneur, according to Paulson. In addition, the grandmother is something of a spoiled brat, insisting that she sit in the middle of the back seat, insisting that her cat travel with the family, and ultimately worst of all, insisting that her son drive to an old plantation to which she insists she knows the way. By the time the reader reaches the point in the story at which the grandmother realizes the house is not in Georgia at all but in Tennessee, and the family has had an auto accident, the reader has probably noticed the references to the grandmother dressing like a lady in case she is found dead on the side of

the road, the reference to a town aptly named Toombsboro, the compari-
son of the car to a hearse, and the references to the escaped convict, the
Misfit. When we read that "behind them the line of woods gaped like a
dark open mouth,"[111] it is easy to imagine what will happen to the family
members who are led into the woods, and before long, the grandmother
is indeed a dead lady on the side of the road.

Reacting to reviews of the collection *A Good Man is Hard to Find and
Other Stories* that called it "brutal and sarcastic," O'Connor responded
that the stories were simply realistic in a Christian world view and that
when reviewers portrayed her stories as "horror stories," she was con-
tinually "amused because the reviewer always has hold of the wrong
horror."[112] Instead of seeing the characters rotting away inwardly, readers
instead tend to concentrate on the violence, gore, and unspeakable acts
in the story; O'Connor intended for these elements to get the readers'
attention, not to preoccupy him.

Regardless of O'Connor's intentions, do the grandmother, her grandchildren, her son, and his wife deserve to be gunned down by the Misfit
and his henchmen? Perhaps not, but what they deserve was not the
issue for O'Connor. Instead, the issue for her was the characters' need
of grace and the testing that the grandmother's faith seems to have
never encountered before now. When she realizes who the Misfit is, she
appeals to every quality she thinks he might have within him to spare
her life. She appeals to his sense of propriety, perhaps because he is so
well-mannered ("You wouldn't shoot a lady, would you?"); to his sense
of family pride ("I know you must come from nice people ... You're not a
bit common!"); to any goodness within him ("I know you're a good man
at heart."); and to any desire for money ("I'll give you all the money I've
got!"). Although he has had his henchmen systematically kill all of the
grandmother's family members, one wonders if the Misfit will spare her
life, that is, until she touches him, saying, "Why you're one of my babies.
You're one of my own children!" He then shoots her in the chest three
times, declaring that "she would have been a good woman ... if it had
been somebody there to shoot her every minute of her life." By this statement, the Misfit means that the grandmother is the kind of woman who
has to be coerced into goodness; only when she is in dire straits, such as
having her life threatened, does she act as if she cares for anyone other
than herself. Ironically, at this point, she does not seem to be trying to
convince him to spare her life; instead, she seems to be genuinely concerned for him. She seems to have realized that both she and the Misfit
are "spoiled brats," willful people who always want their own way. As the
Misfit explains, he has been on a spiritual journey of sorts himself and

has turned to a life of crime because he has seen only two choices: if Jesus truly raised the dead, then "it's nothing for you to do but thow away everything and follow Him," and if he did not, then the only pleasure to be gained in life is through "meanness."[113] Still, even after the Misfit murders the grandmother—the ultimate act of controlling someone else—he admits he has found no pleasure in his act.

O'Connor often read this story to audiences, claiming it was one of the few she could get through without laughing, not that the story does not have its humorous moments. She made it clear that she did not see the Misfit as a Christ figure but instead as utterly reprehensible, and some believe that the catalog of occupations the Misfit has been involved in (jobs with the military, as an undertaker, with the railroad, and as a farmer) and experiences he has endured (being in a tornado, seeing a man burned alive, and seeing a woman flogged) should lead us to see him not as an aberration but as representative of all humanity's natural depravity.[114] However, grace is extended even to him through the touch of the grandmother, and some even believe she extends grace to him in her death as she lies on the road with her legs posed as one being crucified. Likewise, a moment of grace is extended to the grandmother in her confrontation with the Misfit. While the grandmother's faith seems simplistic and untested, she does respond with a gesture of love to the Misfit and the recognition that she is no better than he is. In fact, she claims he is "one of [her] own children,"[115] even though she is fully aware he has had her family murdered; she may be hypocritical and annoying, but many readers believe that her faith ultimately passes the test. The Misfit, on the other hand, is a much more complex character, a man who has been imprisoned for a crime he says he cannot remember committing and who cannot accept by faith that Christ was who he said he was. Instead, he is going through life angry at a world where he is asked to *believe* on faith and was not given the opportunity to live during Christ's day so that he could *see* for himself the type of man Christ really was.

Some have claimed that the Misfit finds no pleasure in killing the grandmother because he knows he is sending her to heaven; however, his frustrated search for truth and justice in the world seems to prove otherwise. Instead, he seems to realize that all the meanness he can muster cannot fill the emptiness inside of him any more than the good works of Sheppard can fill him up, yet he continues to repeat that there is no pleasure in life except meanness, as if to convince himself. Madison Jones contests that pride is as much an issue for the Misfit as it is for the grandmother: "Given his image of himself, her words and her touching, blessing him, amount to an intolerable insult, for hereby she includes him with herself among the world's family of vulgarians, the multitude who can live their lives without ever once asking why. . . . One of her kind, indeed!"[116]

Still other critics believe that there is no hope for redemption offered in this story, despite O'Connor's statements to the contrary. In fact, Stephen Bandy believes, "Its message is profoundly pessimistic and in fact subversive to the doctrines of grace and charity, despite heroic efforts to disguise that fact."[117] According to Bandy, the grandmother's touching the Misfit is nothing more than a last-ditch effort to save herself, and since she has resorted to every other ploy she can think of, she pulls her last weapon out of the bag: motherhood. Bandy writes, "Could this unspeakable act of selfishness carry within it the seeds of grace, acting, as it were, above the Grandmother? So Flannery O'Connor believed. But what is the precise movement of grace in this scene? It is surely straining the text to propose that the Grandmother has in this moment 'seen the light.'"[118] On the other hand, Bandy fails to note the change in the Grandmother just before her last utterance to the Misfit that many believe indicate she has indeed had an epiphany: "the grandmother's head cleared for an instant."[119] This one moment may be enough to reveal to her who she truly is—no better than the Misfit in her true lack of belief and her need of grace. At least, this is what O'Connor would desire us to believe.

O'Connor felt she had not just a message worth hearing but *the* message worth hearing, and she was willing to go to any lengths to get her readers' attention, including humor, violence, and grotesque characters, despite any reservations her readers might have about her methods. If readers were to do as she wished, they would approach all her stories as she would have liked readers to approach "A Good Man is Hard to Find": "be on the lookout for such things as the action of grace . . . and not for the dead bodies."[120]

NOTES

1. Franz Levering, "The Visionary Heart," *Atlanta Gazette*, February 19, 1975, p. 13.

2. Flannery O'Connor, "The Regional Writer," *Mystery and Manners: Occasional Prose*, ed. Sally and Robert Fitzgerald (New York: Farrar, Straus, and Giroux, 1969), p. 55.

3. Margaret Shannon, "The World of Flannery O'Connor," *Atlanta Journal and Constitution Magazine*, February 20, 1972, p. 8.

4. Letter to Robie Macauley, May 18, 1955, *The Habit of Being*, ed. Sally Fitzgerald (New York: Farrar, Straus, and Giroux, 1979), p. 81.

5. Letter to Denver Lindley, March 6, 1957, *The Habit of Being*, p. 206.

6. DeVene Harold, unpublished essay, Flannery O'Connor Collection, Georgia College and State University, Milledgeville.

7. William Goyen, "Unending Vengeance," review of *Wise Blood* by Flannery O'Connor, *New York Times Book Review*, May 18, 1952, p. 4.

8. Joe Lee Davis, "Outraged, or Embarrassed," review of *Wise Blood* by Flannery O'Connor, *Kenyon Review* 15, no. 1: 320–25.

9. Quoted in Joel Wells, "A Genius Who Frustrated Critics," review of *Flannery O'Connor: The Complete Stories*, by Flannery O'Connor, *National Catholic Reporter*, November 19, 1971.

10. Sarah J. Foder, "Marketing Flannery O'Connor: Institutional Politics and Literary Evaluation," rpt. in *Flannery O'Connor: New Perspectives*, ed. Sura P. Rath and Mary Neff Shaw (Athens: University of Georgia Press, 1996), p. 12.

11. Flannery O'Connor, *Wise Blood, Collected Works*, ed. Sally Fitzgerald (New York: Library of America, 1988), pp. 29, 59, 31.

12. Jean W. Cash, *Flannery O'Connor: A Life* (Knoxville: University of Tennessee Press, 2002), p. 25.

13. Sylvia Zsuffa, review of *A Good Man is Hard to Find*, by Flannery O'Connor, *Bulletin of the Catholic Laymen's Association of Georgia*, March 3, 1956.

14. Review of *A Good Man is Hard to Find*, by Flannery O'Connor, *Time*, June 6, 1955, p. 114.

15. Foder, "Marketing Flannery O'Connor," pp. 13, 17.

16. O'Connor, *The Violent Bear It Away, Collected Works*, pp. 473, 479.

17. Marsh Maslin, "A Small-Boy Hero Unique to Fiction," review of *The Violent Bear It Away*, by Flannery O'Connor, *San Francisco News*, February 26, 1960.

18. B. J. Morgan, "Potentiality for Greatness: 'The Violent Bear It Away' Exciting New Fiction Effort," *Arkansas Gazette*, July 24, 1960.

19. Donald Davidson, "A Prophet Went Forth," review of *The Violent Bear It Away*, by Flannery O'Connor, *New York Times*, February 28, 1960.

20. Vivian Mercier, review of *The Violent Bear It Away*, by Flannery O'Connor, *Hudson Review* 13, no. 3: 455.

21. Frank Bigley, "Back South with Too Much Despair," review of *The Violent Bear It Away*, by Flannery O'Connor, *Daily Star* (Montreal, Canada), April 16, 1960.

22. "God-Intoxicated Hillbillies," review of *The Violent Bear It Away*, by Flannery O'Connor, *Time*, February 29, 1960.

23. "Of Ultimate Things," review of *Everything that Rises Must Converge*, by Flannery O'Connor, *Time*, June 4, 1965, p. 92.

24. Irving Howe, "Flannery O'Connor's Stories," review of *Everything that Rises Must Converge*, by Flannery O'Connor, *New York Review of Books*, September 30, 1965, p. 16.

25. "Flannery O'Connor," *Talk of the Nation*, hosted by Melinda Penkava, Natl. Public Radio, May 22, 1997.

26. O'Connor, "Catholic Novelists and Their Readers," *Mystery and Manners*, p. 176.

27. O'Connor, *Wise Blood, Collected Works*, p. 38.

28. Flannery O'Connor, "Good Country People," *A Good Man is Hard to Find and Other Stories* (San Diego: Harcourt, 1983), p. 195.

29. O'Connor, "The Church and the Fiction Writer," *Mystery and Manners*, p. 151.

30. Richard Oxman, "The Violent Bear It Away: Flannery Will Get You Somewhere," *Press Action*, August 21, 2004, http://www.pressaction.com/news/weblog/full_article/oxman08202004/.

31. O'Connor, "Novelist and Believer" and "Catholic Novelists and Their Readers," *Mystery and Manners*, pp. 165, 180.

32. Paul J. Halliman, "Archbishop's Notebook," *Georgia Bulletin*, August 6, 1964.

33. "An Interview with Flannery O'Connor," Interview with Katherine Fugin, Raye Rivard, and Margaret Sieh, *Censer* (Fall 1960): 28–30. Rpt. in *Conversations with Flannery O'Connor*, ed. Rosemary M. Magee (Jackson: University Press of Mississippi, 1987), p. 60.

34. Rebecca R. Butler, "What's So Funny About Flannery O'Connor?" *The Flannery O'Connor Bulletin* 9 (1980): 36.

35. O'Connor, "A Good Man is Hard to Find," *A Good Man is Hard to Find and Other Stories*, p. 19.

36. O'Connor, "The Life You Save May Be Your Own," *A Good Man is Hard to Find and Other Stories*, p. 59.

37. O'Connor, "Parker's Back," *Collected Works*, ed. Sally Fitzgerald (New York: Library of America, 1988), p. 663.

38. O'Connor, "Good Country People," *A Good Man is Hard to Find and Other Stories*, p. 171.

39. O'Connor, "A Good Man is Hard to Find," *A Good Man is Hard to Find and Other Stories*, p. 15.

40. O'Connor, "Revelation," *Collected Works*, p. 640.

41. O'Connor, "The Life You Save May Be Your Own," *A Good Man is Hard to Find and Other Stories*, p. 67.

42. O'Connor, "A Circle in the Fire," *Collected Works*, p. 234.

43. O'Connor, "The Lame Shall Enter First," *Collected Works*, p. 611.

44. O'Connor, Address, Georgia State College for Women, January 7, 1960.

45. Ralph C. Wood, *The Comedy of Redemption: Christian Faith and Comic Vision in Four American Novelists* (Notre Dame, IN: University of Notre Dame Press, 1988), p. 80.

46. Letter to John Lynch, November 6, 1955, *The Habit of Being*, p. 114.

47. Robert Donner, "She Writes Powerful Fiction," *The Sign* 40 (March 1961): 46–48. Rpt. in *Conversations with Flannery O'Connor*, ed. Magee, p. 45.

48. Letter to Alfred Corn, May 30, 1962, *The Habit of Being*, p. 477.

49. Wood, *The Comedy of Redemption*, p. 87.

50. Wood, *The Comedy of Redemption*, p. 89.

51. O'Connor, "Good Country People," *A Good Man is Hard to Find and Other Stories*, pp. 174–75.

52. Sheldon Currie, "Freaks and Folks: Comic Imagery in the Fiction of Flannery O'Connor," *Antigonish Review* 62–63 (1985): 133–42. Rpt. in Suzanne Morrow Paulson, *Flannery O'Connor: A Study of the Short Fiction* (Boston: Twayne, 1988), p. 208.

53. O'Connor, "Good Country People," *A Good Man is Hard to Find and Other Stories*, pp. 186, 194, 195.

54. Frederick Asals, "The Double," *Flannery O'Connor: The Imagination of Extremity.* (Athens: University of Georgia Press, 1982). Rpt. in *Modern Critical Views: Flannery O'Connor,* ed. Harold Bloom (New York: Chelsea House Publishers, 1986), p. 101.

55. Clinton W. Trowbridge, "The Comic Sense of Flannery O'Connor: Literalist of the Imagination," *The Flannery O'Connor Bulletin* 12 (Autumn 1983): 78.

56. Jeanne Campbell Reesman, "Women, Language, and the Grotesque in Flannery O'Connor and Eudora Welty," rpt. in *Flannery O'Connor: New Perspectives*, ed. Rath, p. 46.

57. O'Connor, "The Lame Shall Enter First," *Collected Works,* p. 609.

58. O'Connor, "The Lame Shall Enter First," *Collected Works,* p. 632.

59. Paulson, *Flannery O'Connor: A Study of the Short Fiction,* p. 23.

60. Sister Mariella Gable, "But First It Must Rise," review of *Everything that Rises Must Converge,* by Flannery O'Connor, *The Critic* 23, no. 6 (June/July 1965): 59.

61. Robert Coles, "Teaching Flannery O'Connor," *Flannery O'Connor: In Celebration of Genius,* ed. Sarah Gordon (Athens, GA: Hill Street Press, 2000), p. 13.

62. Joyce Carol Oates, "The Visionary Art of Flannery O'Connor," *Southern Humanities Review* 7, no. 3 (Summer 1973). Rpt. in *Modern Critical Views: Flannery O'Connor,* ed. Bloom, p. 46.

63. O'Connor, "Revelation," *Collected Works,* pp. 637, 639.

64. O'Connor, "Revelation," *Collected Works,* pp. 636, 642.

65. O'Connor, "Revelation," *Collected Works,* pp. 644, 646.

66. O'Connor, "Revelation," *Collected Works,* pp. 647, 651.

67. O'Connor, "Revelation," *Collected Works,* pp. 652–53.

68. Wood, *The Comedy of Redemption,* p. 130.

69. O'Connor, "Revelation," *Collected Works,* p. 654.

70. Wood, *The Comedy of Redemption,* p. 131.

71. Maurice Lévy, "L'écriture catholique de Flannery O'Connor," *Revue française d'études américaines,* trans. C. Frederick Farrell, Jr. and Edith R. Farrell. Rpt. in Paulson, *Flannery O'Connor: A Study of the Short Fiction,* pp. 158–59.

72. O'Connor, "Parker's Back," *Collected Works,* p. 655.

73. Vigen Guroian, "The Tattooed Christ: 'Parker's Back' and the Christian Humanism of Flannery O'Connor," http://www.breakpoint.org/Breakpoint/ChannelRoot/ColumnsGroup/VigenGuroian/The+Tattooed+Christ.htm

74. O'Connor, "Parker's Back," *Collected Works*, p. 655.

75. O'Connor, "Parker's Back," *Collected Works*, p. 669.

76. Dan Curley, "Flannery O'Connor and the Limitless Nature of Grace," *Revista de letras* 7 (1970): 371–84. Rpt. in Paulson, *Flannery O'Connor: A Study of the Short Fiction*, p. 161.

77. O'Connor, "Parker's Back," *Collected Works*, p. 665.

78. O'Connor, "Parker's Back," *Collected Works*, pp. 669, 672.

79. O'Connor, "Parker's Back," *Collected Works*, p. 673.

80. John F. Desmond, *Risen Sons: Flannery O'Connor's Vision of History* (Athens: University of Georgia Press, 1987), p. 78.

81. O'Connor, *Wise Blood, Collected Works*, pp. 9–11.

82. O'Connor, *Wise Blood, Collected Works*, pp. 34, 36.

83. O'Connor, *Wise Blood, Collected Works*, pp. 5, 16–17.

84. O'Connor, *Wise Blood, Collected Works*, p. 59.

85. Frederick Hoffman, *The Art of Southern Fiction: A Study of Some Modern Novelists* (Carbondale: Southern Illinois University Press, 1967), p. 86.

86. Laura B. Kennelly, "Exhortation in *Wise Blood*: Rhetorical Theory as an Approach to Flannery O'Connor," rpt. in *Flannery O'Connor: New Perspectives*, ed. Rath, pp. 164–65.

87. Hoffman, *The Art of Southern Fiction*, p. 88.

88. Debra A. Moddelmog, *Readers and Mythic Signs: The Oedipus Myth in Twentieth-Century Fiction* (Urbana: Southern Illinois University Press, 1993), p. 94.

89. Patricia Yaeger, "Flannery O'Connor and the Aesthetics of Torture," rpt. in *Flannery O'Connor: New Perspectives*, ed. Rath, p. 185.

90. Anthony DiRenzo, *American Gargoyles: Flannery O'Connor and the Medieval Grotesque* (Carbondale: University of Southern Illinois Press, 1995), p. 8.

91. O'Connor, "Some Aspects of the Grotesque in Southern Fiction," *Mystery and Manners*, p. 44.

92. O'Connor, "The Fiction Writer and His Country," *Mystery and Manners*, p. 34.

93. J.M.G. Le Clézio, preface to *Et ce sont les violents qui l'emportent*, Editions Gallimard, trans. C. Frederick Farrell, Jr. and Edith R. Farrell. Rpt. in Paulson, *Flannery O'Connor: A Study of the Short Fiction*, p. 170.

94. O'Connor, Address, Georgia State College for Women, January 7, 1960.

95. Fred Chappell, "Vertigo," in *Flannery O'Connor: In Celebration of Genius*, ed. Sarah Gordon (Athens, GA: Hill Street Press, 2000), p. 28.

96. O'Connor, "A Memoir of Mary Ann," *Collected Works*, p. 822.

97. O'Connor, "A Memoir of Mary Ann," *Collected Works*, pp. 824, 828, 830–31.

98. O'Connor, "A Memoir of Mary Ann," *Collected Works*, pp. 829–30.

99. Gilbert H. Muller, "Flannery O'Connor and the Catholic Grotesque," in *Literary Theories in Praxis*, ed. Shirley F. Staton (Philadelphia: University of Pennsylvania Press, 1987), p. 123.

100. Ronald Weber, "A Good Writer is Hard to Find," *Catholic Dossier* 5, no. 4 (July–August 1999): 31.

101. Anne Elizabeth Carson, "'Break forth and wash the slime from this earth!': O'Connor's Apocalyptic Tornadoes," *Southern Quarterly* 40, no. 1 (Fall 2001): 21.

102. Houston A. Baker, Martha Banta, Nina Baym, Scayan Bercovitch, Emory Elliott, Terence Martin, David Minter, Marjorie Perloff, and Daniel B. Shea, *Columbia Literary History of the United States* (New York: Columbia University Press, 1988), p. 783.

103. Robin Darling Young, "Flannery O'Connor: *The Collected Works*," *First Things First* 101 (March 2000): 59.

104. Granville Hicks, "A Cold, Hard Look at Humankind." *Saturday Review,* May 29, 1965, p. 23.

105. Margaret Whitt, "Flannery O'Connor's Ladies." *The Flannery O'Connor Bulletin* 15 (1986): 48.

106. Hoffman, *The Art of Southern Fiction*, p. 90.

107. Katherine Hemple Prown, *Revising Flannery O'Connor: Southern Literary Culture and the Problem of Female Authorship* (Charlottesville: University Press of Virginia, 2001), p. 50.

108. Wood, *The Comedy of Redemption*, p. 84.

109. O'Connor, "Revelation," *Collected Works*, p. 646.

110. O'Connor, "A Good Man is Hard to Find," *A Good Man is Hard to Find and Other Stories*, p. 15.

111. O'Connor, "A Good Man is Hard to Find," *A Good Man is Hard to Find and Other Stories*, p. 21.

112. Letter to "A," July 20, 1955, *The Habit of Being*, p. 90.

113. O'Connor, "A Good Man is Hard to Find," *A Good Man is Hard to Find and Other Stories*, pp. 22–24, 28.

114. Paul W. Nisly, "The Mystery of Evil: Flannery O'Connor's Gothic Power," *Flannery O'Connor Bulletin* 11 (Autumn 1982): 28–29.

115. O'Connor, "A Good Man is Hard to Find," *A Good Man is Hard to Find and Other Stories*, p. 29.

116. Madison Jones, "O'Connor and Current Fiction," in *Flannery O'Connor: In Celebration of Genius*, ed. Gordon, p. 62.

117. Stephen C. Bandy, "'One of my babies': The Misfit and the Grandmother," *Studies in Short Fiction* 33, no. 1 (Winter 1996): 107.

118. Bandy, "'One of my babies,'" p. 107.

119. O'Connor, "A Good Man is Hard to Find," *A Good Man is Hard to Find and Other Stories*, p. 29.

120. O'Connor, "A Reasonable Use of the Unreasonable," *Mystery and Manners*, p. 113.

Flannery O'Connor at age 3. Courtesy of the Flannery O'Connor Collection, Ina Dillard Russell Library, Georgia College and State University, Milledgeville.

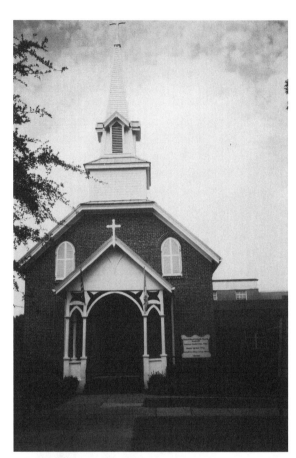

Sacred Heart Catholic Church
After moving to Milledgeville in 1938, the O'Connors regularly attended Sacred Heart Catholic Church. Flannery O'Connor's funeral was held at Sacred Heart on August 4, 1964. Photo by the author.

Cline-O'Connor House
In 1938, O'Connor's family moved to Milledgeville into the family's house (the Gordon-Ward-Beal-Cline-O'Connor House) on Greene Street. Commonly known as the Cline-O'Connor house, the structure was built in 1837. O'Connor's family lived there with her mother's two unmarried sisters, Mary and Katie Cline. Photo by the author.

Georgia College (then Georgia State College for Women) held a book-signing party for O'Connor in 1952 upon the publication of *Wise Blood*. Courtesy of the Flannery O'Connor Collection, Ina Dillard Russell Library, Georgia College and State University, Milledgeville.

Flannery O'Connor in 1961 on the porch of the Cline-O'Connor House. Courtesy of the Flannery O'Connor Collection, Ina Dillard Russell Library, Georgia College and State University, Milledgeville.

Andalusia

After O'Connor's lupus diagnosis, she and her mother moved to Andalusia, a 544-acre farm that is approximately four miles north of Milledgeville. Her mother inherited the farm jointly with her brother Louis Cline from their uncle, but she managed the property virtually alone. O'Connor's bedroom was on the front of the main house on the downstairs level so that she could avoid climbing the stairs. Andalusia was open for public tours in 2003. Photos by the author.

Water Tower at Andalusia
The property at Andalusia contains many structures other than the main house, including a water tower. Photo by the author.

Barn at Andalusia
The barn at Andalusia appears to have been the model for barns in several of O'Connor's stories, including the well-known "Good Country People." Photo by the author.

O'Connor's Grave
Flannery O'Connor died at age 39 on August 3, 1964, from complications of lupus, and she was buried next to her father in Memory Hill Cemetery. Her mother, who died in 1995, was buried near her as well. Photo by the author.

Chapter 4

THE SOUTHERN SCENE

Because of the brilliance of her work and its unusual combination of humor, violence, and theology, it is likely that Flannery O'Connor would have carved a niche in the literary and cultural world no matter where she lived and wrote. But the fact remains that she was from the South, she lived most of her life in the South, and her work is permeated with Southern life and idiom. At age 21, she felt sure that she could not thrive as a writer in the South, and she spent two years in Iowa and then about a year in Connecticut. While she was away from her home in the South, she often socialized with Southerners, but her work bears the stamp of someone trying to shed the locales of her past. As previously mentioned, Virginia Wray notes that prior to *Wise Blood*, the settings in O'Connor's fiction are vague, with nothing distinctly Southern about them. It seems that O'Connor felt trapped by the South, but she slowly began to see its value as part of who she was as a writer. Eventually, her work turned to it, and she never looked back, calling it a "great blessing ... to find at home what others have to go elsewhere seeking."[1]

As discussed earlier, O'Connor's lupus diagnosis necessitated a perma- nent return South, and she clearly dealt with her disease, knowing its ravages from her own father's battle with it. In addition, "it is clear from her correspondence that she cherished her life there and knew that she had been brought back exactly where she belonged and where her best work would be done."[2] Many readers and critics have tried to compartmen- talize her work as part of the school of Southern Degeneracy, Southern Gothic, Fugitive/Agrarian, and so forth, and no matter what group she is placed in, one can always find evidence placing her in a different, even opposite, group. O'Connor hated being pigeonholed, saying to a GSCW audience in 1960, "... while there are no genuine schools in American letters today, there is always some critic who has just invented one and who is ready to put you into it."[3] While she did not want her work to be compartmentalized, she treasured the South's uniqueness and lamented that the angst many Southern writers felt was not from being alienated from other regions of America but because the South was "not alienated enough, that every day we are getting more and more like the rest of the country."[4] Even though she is not a true fit for the Fugitive/Agrarian school, O'Connor was heavily influenced in many ways by those of the movement whom she came to know in Iowa: Andrew Lytle, Robert Penn Warren, Allen Tate, and Caroline Gordon Tate. Famous for their treatise *I'll Take My Stand*, which articulated their philosophical base, the Agrarians felt that the "Old South" should be a model for the rest of America in its reverence for rural life. In other words, "the experience, heritage and values of the Old South should provide for both the North and the South a critical humanizing corrective to the popular notion of limitless progress and directionless development."[5] However, O'Connor did not agree with the Agrarians that the South could be made into an utopia if it were only liberated from machination and industrialization, because woven within this issue was the South's history of marginalizing blacks and women. O'Connor struggled with these very concerns as the Civil Rights Movement was born and as she dealt with her own gender as it related to her identity as a writer.

SOUTHERN WOMANHOOD

According to O'Connor, the focus of her work was the entire human race, and she used the South as a means of portraying and discussing it since she knew the South better than any other place in the world. As she once stated in an interview, "I'm interested in the old Adam. He just talks southern because I do."[6] Regina O'Connor was fervent in her desire for her daughter to be a proper Southern woman, but O'Connor rebelled against her mother's wishes to a certain degree. While she did attend teas given in her honor by Milledgeville ladies after the publication of her books, she disliked doing so and resisted conventional Southern womanhood by doing such things as wearing a sweatshirt with a bulldog and the word "Georgia" on the front—not exactly proper dress for a Southern lady.

In addition, O'Connor did not utilize in her stories the traditional, sentimentalized South of proper ladies sipping mint juleps on the front porch of the plantation home while the men oversee happy slaves in the

fields and the scent of magnolias wafts through the air. Instead, her stories contain many "real" women who, like her mother, had no husband
or other significant man in their lives, so they were forced to survive in
a "man's world." Again like her mother, many of the women in her stories, for example, Mrs. Cope in "A Circle in the Fire," Mrs. Fox in "The
Enduring Chill," and Mrs. McIntyre in "The Displaced Person," must
oversee male workers, forcing them to uphold the decorum expected of a
"Southern lady" while making a living doing "man's work."

At the same time, many of them defend the Southern hierarchy
because they are fairly high up in it (or aspire to be), and they act the part
of the Southern lady in several ways. First, they must always be "nice."
The clichés that dominate Mrs. Hopewell's conversations in "Good
Country People" are a chief example: "... good country people are the
salt of the earth! Besides, we all have different ways of doing, it takes all
kinds to make the world go 'round. That's life!"[7] Mrs. Wally Hitchcock
offers the same sort of comments to Hazel Motes as they ride on the train
together in *Wise Blood*, spouting such niceties as "there's no place like
home" and "time flies."[8]

In several stories, there is an emphasis on fashion, another concern of
conventional Southern womanhood. For example, while Ruby is not running a farm alone, she still determines the position in the social hierarchy of
each person in the doctor's waiting room based on the shoes they wear. At
the top of the social hierarchy in the doctor's office is the "pleasant woman,"
who is wearing gray and red suede shoes and represents the upper class;
apparently trying to undermine the Southern social hierarchy through her
dress is Mary Grace, who is wearing "Girl Scout shoes." Also present are an
old woman wearing tennis shoes, who is apparently next in the hierarchy,
and the "white trashy mother" who is wearing house shoes that have "black
straw with gold thread braided through them—exactly what you would
have expected her to have on."[9] In another example regarding fashion, Mrs.
McIntyre, in "The Displaced Person," is unsure of how to appropriately
respond to the Guizacs' arrival. Therefore, she dresses in her best, for a
Southern lady would much rather be overdressed than underdressed. In
perhaps the most famous example of this fixation on fashion, we have
the Grandmother in "A Good Man is Hard to Find." In contrast to her
daughter-in-law, who is wearing slacks and has her hair tied up in a green
bandanna, the grandmother dresses as if she is attending a formal event:

> ... the grandmother had on a navy blue straw sailor hat with a
> bunch of white violets on the brim and a navy blue dress with
> a small white dot in the print. Her collars and cuffs were white

organdy trimmed with lace and at her neckline she had pinned a purple spray of cloth violets containing a sachet.

She wears white gloves as well, all to make sure that if she were found on the side of the road, anyone seeing her there "would know at once that she was a lady."[10]

Despite the attention to the language and dress of a Southern lady, the women running farms alone still "can obtain only toleration, but no true respect, from the males upon whom they must depend as a matter of economic necessity...."[11] In essence, they try to be a "lady" while at the same time being the "boss" and actually accomplish neither. Perhaps the best example is Mrs. Cope in "A Circle in the Fire." Her black workers ignore her desire for them to drive the tractor through the gate, and she is determined to preserve her farm through her hard work. However, the three hitchhiking boys put an end to that illusion. Mrs. Pritchard is immediately suspicious of the boys and lets them know that in her facial expressions; therefore, the boys figure out quickly that Mrs. Cope is the one they can manipulate, for she gives off an aura of fear, not of authority. When she "shrieks" at one of them who has dropped a cigarette butt, "Please pick that up. I'm afraid of fires," she explicitly reveals her weakness.[12] As a result, they know they can do whatever they want on her land, including setting her woods on fire, and she is powerless to stop them.

Even the "women of leisure," who appear to have no other job than to preserve Southern respectability for their families, command no respect from their families. For example, the Grandmother's son, Bailey, simply humors her with much groaning on his part, and her grandchildren, John Wesley and June Starr, regularly roll their eyes at the stories she tells. The same goes for Julian's mother in "Everything That Rises Must Converge." Her preoccupation with her appearance (and with Julian's) and with her ancestors who were high on the Southern social ladder annoys Julian and prompts him to roll his eyes and say angrily, "Nobody in the damn bus cares who you are."[13]

Another issue regarding Southern womanhood that finds its way from O'Connor's life to her work is the desire of daughters not to turn into their mothers, even though most of them eventually do. Many of O'Connor's stories take place in a matriarchal household, and the daughters often rebel against this authority. In "A Circle in the Fire," Sally Virginia Cope mocks her mother with her fear of fire, yet when the boys set fire to their land, she does not revel in her mother's worst fear coming true but instead feels a "new unplaced misery" that she shares with her mother.[14] Likewise, Hulga Hopewell sneers at her mother's cliché-filled conversations with Mrs. Freeman, yet when Manley Pointer steals her leg, she becomes her mother and can only respond with empty truisms. No matter how much these women try to create their own identities, they are their mothers after all. The only exception seems to be Mary Grace of "Revelation," who is clearly repulsed by her mother's Southern propriety and does everything to be the opposite of her, such as dressing sloppily and attending a Northern college. Even though she is similar to these other characters who do not want to become like their mothers, she is different in that she never succumbs to that maternal influence. Instead, she loathes everything her mother and Ruby stand for with such vehemence that she throws her book at Ruby, jumps on her, and begins strangling her. The fact that Mary Grace is immediately and forcefully sedated by the doctor comes as no surprise, for in a very real sense, Mary Grace has just assaulted someone physically who, the witnesses would surely say, has not provoked her. However, on a different level, Mary Grace *has* been provoked for years by Ruby, by people like her, and by what they represent. Even Ruby perceives this fact: "There was no doubt ... that the girl did know her, knew her in some intense and personal way, beyond time and place and condition."[15]

Other critics see conflict between fathers and daughters as well, primarily "fathers crushing and silencing the assertive daughter." This could be a literal father; however, fathers rarely appear in O'Connor's stories. Typically, the father is some other patriarchal authority—at times even God himself—and the daughter is often not a biological one but simply a woman who has dared to lay hold of power in a male-dominated world. For example, the boys in "A Circle in the Fire" claim Mrs. Cope's woods for "Gawd" and burn it to the ground to teach her a lesson and show their own power over her. Likewise, in "Good Country People," Manley Pointer may be the agent of God's grace and the person necessary to humble Hulga, but in stealing her leg and abandoning her in the barn, he also brings "a destruction of the daughter's dignity and ability to walk alone."[16] Perhaps the most troubling example occurs in "A View of the Woods," in which Mary Fortune Pitts is abused by her father yet stubbornly defends his right to the woods, an act that ultimately brings about her death at the hands of her own grandfather, who has tried to mold his granddaughter into a miniature, female version of himself. Ironically, this technique backfires, for it is the very quality that the grandfather has encouraged most in his granddaughter—the ability to assert her own will over the will of others—that causes her to begin throwing bottles at him as he closes the deal to sell the property that provides Mary Fortune's family with a view of the woods. As he prepares to beat Mary Fortune and punish her for her behavior, the old man thinks, ". . . when he finished with her, she would never throw another bottle again."[17] Ironically, he is correct in this assessment, for she will not relent to his desire to beat her, and they eventually kill each other.

Clearly, the issue of gender in general in O'Connor's work is a complex one, one about which many books and articles have been written. However, from the limited attention we are able to devote to it here, O'Connor seems to be saying that society does not respond favorably to such unconventional ideas or the behavior that becomes with them. It is much easier to silence the nonconformist than it is to tolerate difference. Hence, Mary Grace is not commended for her insight into Ruby Turpin's character and into social conventions of the South; instead, she is sedated, called crazy, and taken away.

Could O'Connor have been using characters such as Mary Grace to comment on the constraints she felt as a Southern woman writer? More than once, O'Connor mentioned the similarities of characters such as Hulga Hopewell and Mary Grace to herself, at least to some degree. Even Mary Grace's clothing, with her "Girl Scout shoes and heavy socks,"[18] is reminiscent of the kinds of outfits O'Connor would wear to irritate her mother, and certainly O'Connor must have faced the temptation of becoming a bitter intellectual because of the position into which her illness drove her.

However, irritating one's mother is one thing; O'Connor's status as a female Southern writer is quite another. Prown maintains that the gender and racial structures that governed the South, especially as they were defined by the literary establishment of the time, mandated that O'Connor masculinize her work if she wanted to be taken seriously as an artist. She was stuck between the proverbial rock and a hard place: high up in the social hierarchy of Milledgeville because of her ancestry yet part of a literary "subculture" because she was a woman writer. Prown also suggests that as O'Connor grew as a writer while she was at Iowa, she quickly realized that the interesting, strong, likeable female characters found in her early writings would have to go. Instead, Prown claims that O'Connor mocks her female characters for "their mistaken pride, [and chastises] them for their domineering ways."[19] Louise Westling tends to agree, placing both Eudora Welty and O'Connor at "the heart of the privileged minority who dominated the South's economic life and preserved its heroic masculine myth of the Lost Cause."[20]

SOUTHERN HISTORY

O'Connor's work does not deal directly with Southern history as such a great deal. As discussed elsewhere, she does explore issues that have a certain Southern flavor to them, such as gender roles and race. However, in very few stories does she explore Southern issues other than these, which may seem odd since she is characterized as a Southern writer. It seems that O'Connor simply found Southern issues, especially the definitive Southern event, the Civil War, to be incredibly boring. In one story, however, she uses this very event to explore much deeper issues that are more common to her work.

In the story "A Late Encounter with the Enemy," O'Connor uses the Civil War and two of the primary Southern stereotypes for the purposes of her story. General George Poker Sash, renamed General Tennessee Flintrock Sash, is a 104-year-old Confederate soldier for whom living is simply a "habit."[21] The General is habitually put on display by his self-consumed granddaughter Sally Poker Sash for Confederate Memorial Day, her college graduation, and any other occasion at which Sally wants to boost her self-image by association with "Southern history." Despite his age and frailty, General Sash represents the ideal male in the South—"the Southern Confederate soldier[,] a model of masculine potency in spite of the reality of defeat"[22]—and his doing so allows him to differentiate himself from others around him while finding an identity in a pivotal event of Southern history. Of course, this representation is a false one, for he cannot even remember the Civil War, much less his actual role in it; Sally claims he was only a Major, though we doubt he was anything more than a common soldier. In fact, the General can remember none of the important events or people in his life—not the death of his son, not his actual role in the Civil War, not his wife. The one event he sees as pivotal in his life is a farce: the day he received a Confederate uniform to wear at a movie premiere. He has lived so long off of history without any genuine sense of its meaning that it is nothing more than a final enemy he battles before his death; he is little more than an artifact to be placed on display. In fact, Desmond has commented that the creation of this image that General Sash embodies is nothing more than his and his granddaughter's "impulse to romanticize history."[23] O'Connor's message seems to be echoed in the statement made by the commencement speaker in the story: "If we forget our past, we won't remember our future and it will be as well for we won't have one." The General has truly forgotten his past and, therefore, forgotten who he is. When the commencement speaker's words reawaken this self-knowledge, he resists it with all he has, even going so far as to "[clench his] sword until the blade touched bone,"[24] and fights it, literally, to the death.

By the same token, Sally Poker Sash represents the Southern belle, who is a "model of feminine purity."[25] This representation is also false, for Sally Poker Sash is filled with nothing if not guile, as she prays every night that her grandfather will live long enough to see her graduate from college, which she has been attending every summer for 20 years. Under different circumstances, this request might be an honorable one; however, she is not concerned that her grandfather live a long life. Rather, she simply wants to share in the status he carries with him. Despite her devious ways, she is intelligent enough to align herself with a powerful societal class by allying herself with her grandfather. According to Paulson, "especially in the South, conformity to the standards and practices of the group is crucial to a sense of well-being."[26] Like her grandfather, however, she seeks to distinguish herself from the group at large by finishing her college degree at age 62. In her mind, getting a degree is not about furthering her knowledge. Instead, it is about status, and this status will have no meaning if the General dies before her graduation, which would keep the status of earning a degree from being coupled with the General's status as a Confederate war hero.

Both characters have an "us vs. them" mentality, much like what we encounter in terms of war. For example, Sally also feels that her earning a college degree is a "mild revenge" against those who have forsaken tradition and redefined Southern living, "upstarts who had turned the world on its head and unsettled the ways of decent living."[27] Like Ruby Turpin and others, this sense of personal significance is fleeting for Sally and the General because it relies on differentiating themselves from others, which actually alienates them from the community of which they wish to be a part. Even then, their alliance to the Old South is proven false as they are lost in the crowd. For example, at the movie premiere, Sally practically jerks the General off the stage after he is introduced by a Hollywood type and is allowed to tell his age. He wants to talk more to the crowd about his formula for youth (kissing "all the pretty guls"),[28] but as another celebrity is brought up on stage, the General and Sally are quickly forgotten. Even at her graduation, as Sally is basking in the perceived glory of her diploma and of her Boy Scout nephew John Wesley escorting the General on stage, she has no idea that the General is already dead as John Wesley speeds him in his wheelchair down a rocky path toward the Coke machine. Clearly, instead of focusing on the vision of the South that she saw as a myth, O'Connor instead focused on what she saw as the *real* South: the landscape, the idiom, the social classes are all there, with every character a representation of some segment of humanity in need of grace.

RACE

The single most discussed aspect of O'Connor's work that relates to its Southern locale is surely the issue of race. The discussion is not so much about O'Connor's exploration of racial issues but her perceived *lack* of appropriate attention to these issues that were so pivotal to the society in which she lived. During her most productive years, racial concerns were the focal point of American society. The *Brown* v. *Board of Education of Topeka, Kansas* court case in 1954 altered the make up of public schools in the South by stating that segregation was unconstitutional. In 1955, 14-year-old Emmett Till was murdered in Mississippi for supposedly whistling at a white woman, and Rosa Parks unwittingly started the Montgomery Bus Boycott by refusing to give up her seat in the white section of the bus. Central High School in Little Rock, Arkansas, was forcefully integrated in 1957, precipitating a call by President Dwight Eisenhower to federal troops and the National Guard to prevent violence against the students, also known as the Little Rock Nine, who integrated the school. In 1960 students at a segregated Greensboro, North Carolina, Woolworth's lunch counter set in motion the "sit-in" movement. Montgomery, Alabama, Commissioner of Public Safety Eugene "Bull" Connor used water hoses and police dogs to attack black protesters in 1963, and also in 1963 were the murder of NAACP official Medgar Evers, the March on Washington, and the bombing of Sixteenth Street Baptist Church in Birmingham, Alabama, which resulted in the deaths of four girls who were attending Sunday School. Clearly, O'Connor lived and wrote in the South at the height of the Civil Rights Movement; however, she did not join her contemporaries, such as Eudora Welty, Robert Penn Warren, and William Styron, who expressed their righteous indignation by signing petitions or publicly demonstrating against racial injustice. As a result, many have questioned what they see as an oversight regarding issues of race in her stories. In addition, some have accused her of being a racist herself because of comments made in her letters and because of her lack of social activism.

O'Connor certainly had a heritage of traditional Southern racial attitudes to contend with. The Cline-O'Connor mansion in Milledgeville, in which she and her mother lived before moving to Andalusia, was built by slaves. In addition, according to Cash, O'Connor's mother, whose attitudes certainly would have influenced her daughter, was little better than a benevolent slave master, relying on blacks to help run her farm yet, at the same time, constantly berating them and viewing them as naturally inferior to whites. Most of these attitudes are conveyed through O'Connor's letters in which she describes her mother's distrust of blacks and resentment toward the materially prosperous ones. Additionally, in a letter to Betty Hester, O'Connor quoted her mother as criticizing her by saying, "You talk just like a nigger."[29] On the other hand, Cash also recounts an instance in which one of Regina O'Connor's black workers was injured and she invested a great deal of her time in getting him medical attention.[30] Regina also bailed Shot, one of her black employees, out of jail on numerous occasions for offenses such as driving while intoxicated. One hopes that her actions were rooted in genuine concern for another human being and not protection of an "investment." Robert Coles insists that her concern was authentic, claiming that Regina "worried about them, taught them, encouraged them, exhorted them, and not least, shared her thoughts and sentiments with them," in addition to driving them places and mediating their disagreements with each other and with town officials.[31]

After reading O'Connor's stories and letters, one might conclude that she herself struggled with contradictory attitudes and behaviors of her own. Perhaps the most troubling comments from O'Connor regarding race are in her letters to her close friend Maryat Lee. After her first visit to Andalusia, Lee rode to the Atlanta airport with a black man in his own car. According to Lee, the fact that she was riding in this man's car and not paying him to drive her there "made all the difference" in the South. After their letter exchange regarding the incident, Lee wrote, "Flannery permanently became devil's advocate with me in matters of race, as I was to do with her in matters of religion. Underneath the often ugly caricatures of herself ... I could only believe that she shared with me the sense of frustration and betrayal and impotency over the dilemma of the white South."[32]

Others are not as generous as Lee in their perceptions of O'Connor's racial attitudes. Writers such as Shirley Ann Grau claim that O'Connor should have recognized segregation as part of the evil she wrote about so often and should have attacked it directly instead of viewing blacks with "an indulgent, amused, tolerant attitude ... if they kept in their place."[33] Will Brantley maintains that O'Connor was "officially" opposed to the scheme of racial prejudice that existed in the South but that she "could not find the nerve to violate the conventions of her region."[34] The event

Brantley refers to involved Maryat Lee's offer to set up a meeting between O'Connor and black writer and activist James Baldwin at Andalusia. O'Connor responded that she could not meet with Baldwin because of the commotion that such a visit would cause in Milledgeville: "Might as well expect a mule to fly as me to see James Baldwin in Georgia." O'Connor also made some disparaging remarks about Baldwin in a 1964 letter to Lee in which she wrote the following: "... the kind [of black person] I don't like is the philosophizing prophesying pontificating kind, the James Baldwin kind. Very ignorant but never silent."[35] According to Cash, O'Connor was simply respecting the traditions of the town in which she lived, whether she agreed with them or not. Because of her upbringing, she would have been trained in the importance of treating her town and its Southern traditions with such respect. Therefore, Cash claims that any offensive comments in her personal correspondence were simply facetious and that her stories reflect her true attitude of Christian charity toward blacks.[36] O'Connor also held in disdain arrogant, white, Northern integrationists who thought they knew what was best for the South, whether they had ever lived in the South or not. Therefore, she often made it appear to others that she was less concerned with racial issues than she truly was.

Others, however, maintain that O'Connor wasn't so much concerned with Milledgeville traditions as she was concerned with getting and keeping the approval of the white males who controlled the literary establishment and who believed that "blacks [were] primarily ... the signifiers through which white southern identity was constructed."[37] Since the idealized woman was viewed by Southern literary gurus, such as Cleanth Brooks and Allen Tate, as the bane of nineteenth-century Southern literature, they sought to shift the focus to the idealized *male*, with an emphasis on intellectual and racial superiority. To be a successful writer, O'Connor may have felt that she needed the approval of this group; therefore, she may have focused on her superior status as a *white person*, rather than as a *woman* in order to improve her position in the Southern literary hierarchy.

In her well-known essay "Beyond the Peacock: The Reconstruction of Flannery O'Connor," African-American writer Alice Walker, who lived in Eatonton, which is near Milledgeville, as a child, offers a fairly balanced assessment of O'Connor's comments about blacks. As one might expect, Walker finds many of her comments to be distasteful. However, like Cash, she examines O'Connor's racial attitudes in her stories and maintains that other Southern writers, such as William Faulkner and Carson McCullers, were "obsessed with a racial past that would not let them go." On the other hand, O'Connor did not seem much concerned about the racial past but instead presented all types of people—white Southern "ladies," white men, blacks—in their total humanity, in all of its ugliness. In fact, Walker claims that the fact that O'Connor rarely delved into the inner beings of blacks "seems to me all to her credit," that her approaching black characters with such "unusual humility and restraint" showed what a "mature artist" she was.[38]

In further defense of O'Connor, Ralph C. Wood's examination of her letters in his article "Where Is the Voice Coming from? Flannery O'Connor on Race" notes that many of O'Connor's distasteful comments, such as her reference to wanting to send blacks back to Africa, must be read within the context of O'Connor's life. Many of the most objectionable letters were written in 1964 during her last struggle with lupus, during which time she was in a great deal of pain and would have been understandably irritable, pessimistic, and cynical. In addition, O'Connor grew increasingly frustrated with being considered an expert on race relations simply because she lived in and wrote about the South. In fact, the comment about sending blacks back to Africa was the product of a visit to Washington, D.C., during which O'Connor lectured at Georgetown and was grilled by reporters on the issue of race in the South. As Cash notes, "Since she seldom suffered fools gladly, the strident voices of reporters clearly irritated her."[39]

Wood also maintains that if O'Connor were truly a racist, she, who never cared if others approved of her or not, would have surely expressed her views publicly. Her stories, which reveal so much about who she was, would have inevitably borne out this contradiction of her belief that God's grace is offered to *everyone*. However, just the opposite appears to be true. While O'Connor does employ the use of the word "nigger" liberally in her stories, it comes from the mouths of characters such as Mr. Head in "The Artificial Nigger" who would have most certainly used the word in the vilest way possible in his daily speech. To omit the word from his vocabulary would violate his character. In addition, most of the letters between Lee and O'Connor contain a spirit of mischievousness and of mutual agitation, as O'Connor, "the social conservative whose (usually) playful prodding established her as the devil's advocate of all liberal causes," sought to antagonize Lee, "the social agitator whose principles will not allow her to conform to 'niceness' of social acceptability, especially as defined by Southern culture."[40]

In fact, several O'Connor stories contain positive portrayals of blacks and clear denunciations of racism. For example, in "The Artificial Nigger," the black man that Mr. Head and Nelson see on the train is described as serene, impeccably dressed, almost regal:

> He had on a light suit and a yellow satin tie with a ruby pin in it. One of his hands rested on his stomach which rode majestically under his buttoned coat, and in the other he held the head of a black walking stick that he picked up and set down with a deliberate outward motion each time he took a step.[41]

This man's rich dress and ability to pay to eat in the dining car stand in stark contrast to the much poorer Mr. Head and Nelson, who bring a sack lunch with them and subsequently leave it on the train by mistake. In fact, Mr. Head's view of himself is so inflated that it is almost comical. Descriptions of his shack of a home emphasize his poverty and isolation by mentioning details such as the slop jar and the fact that he and Nelson have to leave the house by 4 a.m. to get to the railroad junction at 5:45 to meet the train stopping especially for them; at the same time, Mr. Head looks at the city as a terrible place, simply because blacks live there. When the almost majestic black man walks through the train, Nelson doesn't even recognize that he has just seen his first black man—a person who is supposed to be the object of his greatest antipathy, a fact which seems to say that racism must be taught. Unfortunately, Mr. Head begins his instruction of Nelson shortly after his first encounter with the black man by loudly insulting the blacks who work on the train.

Furthermore, in stories such as "The Enduring Chill" and "Revelation," we see examples of "signifying"—blacks offering feigned praise in order to ridicule whites. In "Revelation," for example, Ruby recounts to the black employees on her farm the story of Mary Grace hitting her with the book and calling her an "old wart hog from hell," and the blacks respond with indignation:

> "Lemme see her. I'll kill her!"
>
> "I'll kill her with you!" the other one cried.
>
> "She b'long in the sylum," the old woman said emphatically. "You the sweetest white lady I know."
>
> "She pretty too," the other two said. "Stout as she can be and sweet. Jesus satisfied with her!"
>
> "Deed he is," the old woman declared.[42]

Recognizing it as nothing more than flattery, Ruby is enraged by their remarks, yet she is rendered powerless and does nothing but offer them water to drink. It is also worth noting that O'Connor's work includes numerous portrayals of self-absorbed whites who are totally dependent on blacks, such as Mrs. McIntyre in "The Displaced Person." Even at the end of "Everything that Rises Must Converge," Julian's mother calls out for Caroline, the black nurse of her youth.

"THE ARTIFICIAL NIGGER"

Perhaps O'Connor's clearest condemnation of racism is in the story that gets the most attention because of its title and that O'Connor claimed was her favorite and one of her best: "The Artificial Nigger." Mr. Head, a haughty, spiteful old man, takes his 10-year-old grandson, Nelson, who has never seen a black person, on a "moral mission" to Atlanta in order to break the boy's pride for having been born in the city and to "educate" him about the depravity of the black race. Each just as stubborn as the other and each trying to dominate the other, Mr. Head and Nelson bicker throughout the story, with Mr. Head telling Nelson at the beginning, "The day is going to come ... when you'll find you ain't as smart as you think you are."[43] As one might expect from an O'Connor story, Mr. Head's words come back to haunt him.

Throughout the story, Mr. Head makes a point of humiliating Nelson and any black person he sees, first by announcing on the train that Nelson has just seen his first black man. As Paulson notes, he objectifies blacks in order to assert his power over them, making such statements as " 'What [not who] was that?' and exclaims to a fellow passenger, 'That's his first nigger,' as if the encounter was like getting a first bicycle."[44] Next, Mr. Head denigrates the train's black kitchen staff when he is told he cannot come into the kitchen. Like so many of O'Connor's characters, Mr. Head's egotism is evident as he tries to establish himself as the ultimate authority in Nelson's eyes. When the two get lost in Atlanta and end up in a black neighborhood, Mr. Head is too proud to ask a black person for directions, so Nelson chooses the least intimidating person to ask out of an entire neighborhood watching him and his grandfather wander aimlessly: a large black woman wearing a pink dress. Nelson is drawn to her, bringing to light his longings for the mother he never had, and O'Connor's description of the "glistening sweat on her neck" and her "tremendous bosom" is sexual and maternal at the same time.[45] According to Ralph Wood, she is a "black Madonna": a sign of their salvation that neither Nelson nor Mr. Head can publicly acknowledge because of the prevailing social codes.[46] Nevertheless, Nelson "suddenly wanted her to reach down and pick him up and draw him against her ... He wanted to look down and down into her eyes while she held him tighter and tighter."[47]

The woman provides the information they need, but not before she calls Nelson "Sugar pie," nearly causing him to collapse. Now that Nelson has committed what, to his grandfather, is the ultimate indignity by lowering himself to ask a black woman for help, Mr. Head is infuriated and drags him back into a white neighborhood. Then, when Nelson falls asleep, Mr. Head succumbs to the aggression which seems to have been created in him by this fierce competitiveness with Nelson and cruelly leaves him, hiding several feet away so that he can observe Nelson's reaction when he wakes up and finds himself alone. Impatient to teach Nelson a lesson, Mr. Head eventually creates a loud noise, which startles Nelson awake and causes him to run away and collide with an old woman carrying groceries. Nelson turns to his grandfather for support and help as this woman and several others jeer at and threaten him, and Mr. Head responds with a betrayal much like Peter's betrayal of Christ in his moment of crisis at the crucifixion: "This is not my boy.... I never seen him before."[48] Just as those around Peter knew he was a follower of Christ because of his similar accent, the old women know that Nelson belongs to Mr. Head because the two look so much alike. They are so repulsed at his betrayal of Nelson, who is obviously a member of his family, that they leave with little more than some fist shaking.

Realizing what he has done, Mr. Head tries to coax Nelson back to him with a drink of water, but Nelson responds with a glare and "steady hate" that Mr. Head knows will "continue just that way for the rest of his life ... nothing was like it had ever been before, a long old age without respect and an end that would be welcome because it would be the end."[49] Nelson perceives that he now has a weapon to use against his grandfather; according to Wood, "this involuted personal distrust is the primordial ground and root ... of that social distrust which issues in racial hatred."[50] Both want to be completely self-reliant, and each feels he has to beat the other into submission in order to reach this goal. They deny their need for each other, an action which Wood claims has the same root as racism.

The two join together again reluctantly, only because they both want to find the train station and get home, and a pivotal moment occurs for both of them when they end up in an stylish suburb and see the "artificial nigger" in a yard: "It was not possible to tell if the artificial Negro were meant to be young or old; he looked too miserable to be either.

He was meant to look happy because his mouth was stretched up at the corners but the chipped eye and the angle he was cocked at gave him a wild look of misery instead."[51] The statue is a symbol and reminder of the black race's suffering, and it emphasizes to both Mr. Head and Nelson their "common defeat." Mr. Head, his pride deflated, sees himself as he truly is:

> He stood appalled, judging himself with the thoroughness of God, while the action of mercy covered his pride like a flame and consumed it. He had never thought himself a great sinner before but he saw now that his true depravity had been hidden from him lest it cause him despair.... He saw that no sin was too monstrous for him to claim as his own.[52]

For Mr. Head to experience an instant, total transformation would not only be unbelievable, but it would also lower O'Connor's story into that category of sentimental fiction which she detested. Mr. Head's specific attitude toward blacks has yet to be transformed, yet something within him that is much larger than one issue has been moved through this experience, something he will be forced to ponder in the future so that he can comprehend it. While the story focuses on the potential for change in Mr. Head, Nelson is not left untouched, as he speaks "with a strange shivering about his mouth."[53] Richard Giannone offers the following assessment: "Since the ending of the story ["The Artificial Nigger"] does not rush the reader to the barricades of civil protest, the social activist will be disappointed with this version of the South's tragedy.... [yet] Mr. Head's recognition of the need for sharing in the pain and mercy of other persons alters more than a racial attitude. It transforms his view of himself, others, and God."[54] At least we hope.

Other critics disagree with this assessment of the story. According to Paulson, Nelson and Mr. Head do suffer, and through their suffering, they are reunited. However, their suffering is most certainly not the same as what the black race has suffered throughout American history, either in degree or in duration. Paulson states, "Head and Nelson's reunion represents ... a widening in the division between the two races because Nelson adopts his grandfather's ideas."[55] Regardless of one's interpretation, O'Connor's pattern of moving the story from a very specific, regional issue to an issue that applies to all humanity is evident. In this case, she moves from the specific Southern issue of racism to the need for humility and compassion toward all humanity and the need of grace to break the cycle of sin in each individual.

CENSORSHIP

Despite what can be viewed as an anti-racism message in "The Artificial Nigger," it is this very story that has come under censure in recent years, causing O'Connor's works to be banned in several places. In fact, A Good Man is Hard to Find ranks at number 61 on the American Library Association's most banned and/or challenged books of the twentieth century.[56] In a notable example of such action against O'Connor's work, A Good Man is Hard to Find was placed on a summer reading list at Opelousas Catholic School in Louisiana in 2000. Without having read the story but simply unnerved by the title "The Artificial Nigger" and by the grandmother's use of the word "pickaninnies" in "A Good Man is Hard to Find," several parents complained to Fr. Malcolm O'Leary, the pastor of Holy Ghost Catholic Church. According to J. Bottum, O'Leary, who admitted he had not read the stories and said he would not "waste [his] time" doing so, gathered a group of black parents to discuss the problem without inviting the teacher who had assigned the story to the meeting. As a result of the meeting, O'Leary contacted Bishop Edward J. O'Donnell to have the book officially removed from the curriculum and the first-year teacher, Arsenio Orteza, disciplined. While Orteza was not reprimanded, the book was banned from the school's curriculum. Bottum writes the following:

> The story has all the elements you might expect. A Catholic literature teacher who foolishly imagined that his job was merely to teach Catholic literature. A collection of Catholic parents and pastors unfamiliar with even the most famous Catholic figures of their own region. A demand made of Church authorities by the activists of a particular social issue. An uninformed bishop who, faced with those activists, proved incapable of doing anything but feebly rush to assert his own political correctness.[57]

Orteza claimed that, as he taught the story at Opelousas, he wanted to bring out O'Connor's religious beliefs in a way that he had not been able to do when teaching at secular schools in the past, stating, "There has not been any writer in twentieth-century America who has been so able to combine her intelligent love of the Catholic faith with her intelligent love for the craft of writing and so been able to make her convictions enfleshed in her fiction." But these nuances of O'Connor's work remained unexplored at a Catholic school, an irony that Peter Cline, an Atlanta English teacher who is also O'Connor's second cousin, found "delicious."[58] Certainly, O'Connor would have been amused as well.

POLITICS AND ART

One of the reasons O'Connor did not address racial issues more frequently in her stories was that she did not feel that politics and art should mix. That point of view may seem a bit odd coming from O'Connor since this present life must be changed to some degree for the "transfigured life to come" to be changed.[59] But as previously mentioned, O'Connor saw revealing humanity's need for grace and God's desire to supply it in the crucifixion of Christ as the purpose of her work. Therefore, she seemed to view racism as a "sin problem," not a social problem.

In addition, Wood claims that O'Connor felt that discrimination was so obviously immoral that it did not require explicit condemnation. Instead, there was another, less overt problem that many neglected to comment on: O'Connor was repulsed by what she saw as a profusion of self-righteousness among social activists, much like her character Sheppard in "The Lame Shall Enter First." According to Wood, O'Connor simply saw much deeper into the issue than other writers and social activists did: she saw the "spiritual subtleties that the gross moralism of the time was prone to ignore" and exposed the "sins of the supposedly righteous [that] were altogether as egregious as the evils of the obviously wicked" racists.[60] She and other Southern Catholic writers, such as Thomas Merton, harbored a "distrust of white liberals turning a rightful demand for racial justice into a wrongful demand for moral self-congratulation."[61] She seemed to feel that many Northerners saw the racial tensions of the South as a means to exalt their more "enlightened" way of life while denigrating life in the South, which frustrated and angered O'Connor. Her disdain for black activists such as James Baldwin was not based on race but on attitude. In O'Connor's view, Baldwin was an arrogant know-it-all, and she wanted to have nothing to do with him. Conversely, she greatly admired Martin Luther King because of his spiritual genuineness. In other words, she felt that King truly cared about the fate of his race and sacrificed himself to aid his people; Baldwin, on the other hand, cared only about self-promotion. Many Northerners simply came to the South, set on "fixing" a region they saw as "backward," claiming they were here to liberate the black race, and showing that those who come to liberate can be just as haughty and intolerant as those who oppress.

Along with "The Lame Shall Enter First," perhaps O'Connor's most crushing censure of sanctimonious activism is in the story "Everything that Rises Must Converge." In this story, Julian, the college-educated, jobless "writer" who is in constant inner turmoil over the condition of his life in the "backward" South, is paired with his "backward" mother who derives her self-worth from an association with the genteel past of her family, symbolized by slaves that are no more and a plantation that is crumbling, leaving her to live in an apartment in a declining part of town. Julian is a bitter young man who isolates himself from everyone around him, especially his mother, because he thinks he is superior to them and much more enlightened. It seems the ultimate insult to Julian is being forced to escort his mother to her weight loss class at the downtown Y simply because she will not ride alone on an integrated bus. His somewhat childish mother is an embarrassment to Julian as she is so easily pleased by a hideous purple and green hat that she wears "like a banner of her imaginary dignity." He despises what he thinks she stands for—her ideas of superiority based on race and class—yet he is dependent on her and secretly longs for the distinction his mother enjoyed as a young person in an affluent family. This situation causes him to be "saturated in depression, as if in the midst of his martyrdom he had lost his faith."[62] Assessing Julian as narcissistic, immature, and duplicitous, Paulson writes that his "sense of superiority ironically rests on the idea that he is *not* classist or racist."[63] Indeed, "the sin of false righteousness becomes especially pernicious when it is linked with filial ingratitude."[64] Julian may be enlightened, but he is also malicious, while his mother, whose racial attitudes are not exactly what they should be, is nevertheless a kind, charitable person.

Thinking that he is surrounded by idiots and that he can see exactly who his mother is from within the refuge of his high-mindedness, Julian decides to humiliate and, therefore, enlighten her by moving on their bus ride to sit next to a well-dressed black man reading a newspaper. Julian has a regular habit of trying to strike up a conversation with well-dressed, intelligent-looking blacks, and he fails to understand why he has not been able to make many black friends. However, the reaction of this man on the bus explains why: he seems to know immediately that he is being used by Julian to make a statement and that Julian is in no way interested in him as a person but as a pawn in some sort of political game.

Finally, Julian gets what he thinks is a golden opportunity to properly "educate" his mother. When a mean-looking black woman wearing a hat identical to Julian's mother's gets on the bus with her small son, Julian is almost giddy with glee, hoping that his mother will be humiliated. Instead, his mother ignores the hat and plays peek-a-boo with the little boy, while the black woman's anger intensifies by the second. When, in the tradition of the old South in which Julian's mother continues to imagine herself living, she offers the little black boy a penny, the boy's enraged mother shouts, "He don't take nobody's pennies!" and knocks Julian's mother down with her purse. Instead of immediately checking on his mother's physical well being, Julian lectures her about her behavior, saying, "That was the whole colored race which will no longer take your condescending pennies.... What all this means ... is that the old world is gone. The old manners are obsolete and your graciousness is not worth a damn.... You aren't who you think you are."[65] In this moment, Julian thinks he has won—that he has been able to use this experience to dismantle the identity of the mother he finds so offensive.

Immediately after Julian's lecture, his mother staggers down the sidewalk, clearly delusional, calling for Caroline, the black nurse of her youth, and wanting to go "home" to her grandfather's plantation house. As she yearns for these symbols of security and identity, Julian soon learns that he too is not who he thinks he is. He is bitter and angry over his situation in life, over the plantation house that he claims to detest but actually resents because he was never able to enjoy its splendor and status. As his mother collapses on the sidewalk, apparently dead from a stroke, Julian realizes that the one person who truly loved him and sacrificed herself for him, despite his mean-spiritedness, is gone. "He has been so obsessed with casting out the racist mote in his mother's eye that he remains oblivious to the beamlike presumption and ingratitude that afflict his own vision. Julian can 'love' the anonymous Negro whom he does not know, but not the mother whom he does know and who also knows him."[66] As Sarah Gordon notes, "the fiercely proud black woman, the silly but goodhearted mother whose values are dismissed by her educated and 'liberal' son, and the son himself, whose apparently generous spirit is in reality a tangle of vipers—all three constitute O'Connor's retort to those, including Maryat Lee herself, who offer simple solutions to the matter of human imperfection."[67]

As O'Connor also believed, there was no simple solution for the racial conflict which existed in the South. This story was published in 1965, at the height of tension in the South. O'Connor remarked that this story was a deliberate attempt to comment directly on the South's most volatile issue. The story received many negative reviews, however, because it did not present the conventional dichotomy of white vs. black or Old, bigoted South (represented by Julian's mother) vs. New, enlightened South (represented by Julian). In fact, Robert Coles states that activists who wanted changes all across society—economic, societal, political, etc.—wanted these types of "conventional polarities" as a "boost" that the things they were doing in public places such as schools, courthouses, and busses were effecting a "revolution in sensibility."[68] But O'Connor does not provide these polarities. Instead, readers find themselves thinking less and less highly of Julian, who secretly dreams of the life his mother lived as a child and seems to only "choose sides" with Southern blacks because he resents what he sees as a deprivation of status and takes his resentment out on his mother. As Coles notes, Julian says many things that Civil Rights workers said in the 1960s. However, it is this other side of him—the real Julian—that outlasts anything he says in the story.

Those who risked their very lives in the Civil Rights Movement, whites especially, might have been justifiably offended by O'Connor's creation of Julian. No doubt, many were. It is in response to that righteous indignation that Coles responds to the question of what exactly O'Connor was trying to say about integration in this story. Whites can be ridiculous and petty, self-consumed and mean. So can blacks because all are part of the sinful human condition. Perhaps most important, "when the buses are integrated (and everything else once segregated, too) there will be no new Jerusalem of a South, only people who are fairly decent, and people who are rather indecent, and all measure in between. And [O'Connor] more than hints that she is talking about both races."[69]

SOLUTIONS

So if O'Connor did not see integration and the Civil Rights Movement as a whole as the solution to the South's racial dilemma, what kind of solution did she see? As mentioned previously, O'Connor seemed to see prejudice as just another failure of humanity, one that cannot be easily solved with laws, policies, or protests. Just as no one can be forced to love God, no one can be forced to love his neighbor, of any race. Therefore, if change were to come to the South, it had to first take place in the human heart, which could then deal with racial differences with a combination of manners and charity. O'Connor stated the following in a 1963 interview:

> It requires considerable grace for two races to live together, particularly when the population is divided about fifty-fifty between them and when they have our particular history. It can't be done without a code of manners based on mutual charity.... When you have a code of manners based on charity, then when the charity fails—as it is going to do constantly—you've got those manners there to

preserve each race from small intrusions upon the other.... For the rest of the country, the race problem is settled when the Negro has his rights, but for the Southerner, whether he's white or colored, that's only the beginning. The South has to evolve a way of life in which the two races can live together with mutual forebearance. You don't form a committee to do this or pass a resolution; both races have to work it out the hard way.[70]

Clearly, O'Connor believed that the past could not be changed but that impatient methods promoted by most Civil Rights activists would "drive out the devil of injustice, only to welcome in seven new devils of incivility."[71]

Realizing that the racial issues of the South were ingrained into its people, its soil, and its culture, O'Connor knew that there would be no easy solution. Just as she saw faults in the Church she loved so well, she saw faults in the region she loved. In addition, she abhorred the smugness of "outsiders" from the North who wanted to radically change a place with which they were not familiar and in which they had never lived, creating a political circus that would exacerbate racial problems instead of solve them. According to Wood, O'Connor's deepest feelings regarding this sensitive issue are these: "She understood that, severed from charity, both morals and manners are without foundation. Nothing less and nothing other than the grace of God can work the miracle that enables the races not merely to tolerate each other but to live together as redeemed and reconciled brothers and sisters of the same Lord."[72]

NOTES

1. Flannery O'Connor, "The Regional Writer," *Mystery and Manners: Occasional Prose*, ed. Sally and Robert Fitzgerald (New York: Farrar, Straus, and Giroux, 1969), p. 54.

2. Sally Fitzgerald, ed., *The Habit of Being* (New York: Farrar, Straus, and Giroux, 1979), p. xvi.

3. Flannery O'Connor, Address, Georgia State College for Women, January 7, 1960.

4. O'Connor, "The Fiction Writer and His Country," *Mystery and Manners*, pp. 28–29.

5. Lorine M. Getz, *Flannery O'Connor: Her Life, Library and Book Reviews* (New York: Edwin Mellon Press, 1980), p. 34.

6. Gerard E. Sherry, "An Interview with Flannery O'Connor," *The Critic* 21 (June/July 1963): 29–31. Rpt. in *Conversations with Flannery O'Connor*, ed. Rosemary M. Magee (Jackson: University Press of Mississippi, 1987), p. 98.

7. O'Connor, "Good Country People," *A Good Man is Hard to Find and Other Stories*, (San Diego: Harcourt, 1983), p. 179.

8. Flannery O'Connor, *Wise Blood, Collected Works*, ed. Sally Fitzgerald (New York: Library of America, 1988), pp. 3, 6.

9. O'Connor, "Revelation," *Collected Works*, p. 635.

10. O'Connor, "A Good Man is Hard to Find," *A Good Man is Hard to Find and Other Stories*, p. 11.

11. Peter A. Smith, "Flannery O'Connor's Empowered Women," *American Scholar* 26, no. 2 (Spring 1994): 47.

12. O'Connor, "A Circle in the Fire," *Collected Works*, p. 238.

13. O'Connor, "Everything That Rises Must Converge," *Collected Works*, p. 489.

14. O'Connor, "A Circle in the Fire," *Collected Works*, p. 250.

15. O'Connor, "Revelation," *Collected Works*, pp. 645–46.

16. Louise Westling, "Fathers and Daughters in Welty and O'Connor," *The Female Tradition in Southern Literature*, ed. Carol S. Manning (Urbana, IL: University of Chicago Press, 1993), pp. 111, 117.

17. O'Connor, "A View of the Woods," *Collected Works*, p. 543.

18. O'Connor, "Revelation," *Collected Works*, p. 635.

19. Katherine Hemple Prown, *Revising Flannery O'Connor: Southern Literary Culture and the Problem of Female Authorship* (Charlottesville: University Press of Virginia, 2001), p. 45.

20. Westling, "Fathers and Daughters," p. 110.

21. O'Connor, "A Late Encounter with the Enemy," *A Good Man is Hard to Find and Other Stories*, p. 155.

22. Suzanne Morrow Paulson, *Flannery O'Connor: A Study of the Short Fiction* (Boston: Twayne, 1988), p. 29.

23. John F. Desmond, *Risen Sons: Flannery O'Connor's Vision of History*, (Athens: University of Georgia Press, 1987), p. 87.

24. O'Connor, "A Late Encounter with the Enemy," *A Good Man is Hard to Find and Other Stories*, pp. 165–67.

25. Paulson, *Flannery O'Connor: A Study of the Short Fiction*, p. 29.

26. Paulson, *Flannery O'Connor: A Study of the Short Fiction*, p. 47.

27. O'Connor, "A Late Encounter with the Enemy," *A Good Man is Hard to Find and Other Stories*, p. 156.

28. O'Connor, "A Late Encounter with the Enemy," *A Good Man is Hard to Find and Other Stories*, p. 161.

29. Letter to "A," March 24, 1956, *The Habit of Being*, p. 148.

30. Jean W. Cash, *Flannery O'Connor: A Life* (Knoxville: University of Tennessee Press, 2002), pp. 148–49.

31. Robert Coles, *Flannery O'Connor's South* (Baton Rouge: Louisiana State University Press, 1980), p. 48.

32. Maryat Lee, "Flannery, 1957," *The Flannery O'Connor Bulletin* 5 (Autumn 1976): 44–45.

33. Shirley Ann Grau, "The O'Connor Letters: A Good Woman is Hard to Find," review of *The Habit of Being*, ed. by Sally Fitzgerald, *Chicago Tribune*, March 25, 1979.

34. Will Brantley, *Feminine Sense in Southern Memoir: Smith, Glasgow, Welty, Hollman, Porter, and Hurston* (Jackson: University Press of Mississippi, 1993), p. 7.

35. Letters to Maryat Lee, April 25, 1959, and May 21, 1964, *The Habit of Being*, pp. 329, 580.

36. Cash, *Flannery O'Connor: A Life*, p. 152.

37. Prown, *Revising Flannery O'Connor*, p. 4.

38. Alice Walker, "Beyond the Peacock: The Reconstruction of Flannery O'Connor," *In Search of Our Mothers' Gardens* (San Diego: Harcourt, 1984), pp. 52, 59.

39. Cash, *Flannery O'Connor: A Life*, p. 154.

40. Sarah Gordon, "Maryat and Julian and the 'not so bloodless revolution,' " *The Flannery O'Connor Bulletin* 21 (1992), p. 27.

41. O'Connor, "The Artificial Nigger," *Collected Works*, p. 215.

42. O'Connor, "Revelation," *Collected Works*, p. 650.

43. O'Connor, "The Artificial Nigger," *Collected Works*, p. 211.

44. Paulson, *Flannery O'Connor: A Study of the Short Fiction*, p. 78.

45. O'Connor, "The Artificial Nigger," *Collected Works*, p. 223.

46. Ralph C. Wood, "Flannery O'Connor's Racial Morals and Manners," *The Christian Century* 111, no. 33 (November 16, 1994), pp. 1076–81.

47. O'Connor, "The Artificial Nigger," *Collected Works*, p. 223.

48. O'Connor, "The Artificial Nigger," *Collected Works*, pp. 223, 226.

49. O'Connor, "The Artificial Nigger," *Collected Works*, p. 228.

50. Ralph C. Wood, *The Comedy of Redemption: Christian Faith and Comic Vision in Four American Novelists* (Notre Dame, IN: University of Notre Dame Press, 1988), p. 116.

51. O'Connor, "The Artificial Nigger," *Collected Works*, p. 229.

52. O'Connor, "The Artificial Nigger," *Collected Works*, p. 231.

53. O'Connor, "The Artificial Nigger," *Collected Works*, p. 230.

54. Richard Giannone, *Flannery O'Connor and the Mystery of Love* (Urbana, IL: University of Chicago Press, 1989), pp. 88–89.

55. Paulson, *Flannery O'Connor: A Study of the Short Fiction*, p. 81.

56. "Banned and/or Challenged Books from the Radcliffe Publishing Course Top 100 Novels of the 20th Century," http://www.ala.org/ala/pio/piopresskits/bbbwpresskit/bannedchallenged.htm.

57. J. Bottum, "Flannery O'Connor Banned," *Crisis* 18, no. 9 (October 2000): 49.

58. Amy Wellborn, "Flannery O'Connor Banned in Opelousas," *Our Sunday Visitor*, September 10, 2000, http://amywelborn.com/flannery/banned.html.

59. Robert Bain and Joseph M. Flora, *Fifty Southern Writers After 1900: A Bio-Bibliographical Sourcebook* (New York: Greenwood Press, 1987), p. 342.

60. Wood, *The Comedy of Redemption*, p. 108.

61. George Kilcourse, Address, "Thomas Merton and Racism: 'Letters to a White Liberal' Reconsidered," Thomas Merton Society of Great Britain and Ireland, Southampton, England, May 1996, http://pages.britishlibrary.net/thomasmerton/kilcour.htm.

62. O'Connor, "Everything that Rises Must Converge," *Collected Works*, pp. 489, 486.

63. Paulson, *Flannery O'Connor: A Study of the Short Fiction*, p. 82.

64. Wood, *The Comedy of Redemption*, p. 120.

65. O'Connor, "Everything that Rises Must Converge," *Collected Works*, pp. 498–99.

66. Wood, "Flannery O'Connor's Racial Morals and Manners," p. 1079.

67. Gordon, "Maryat and Julian and the 'not so bloodless revolution,'" p. 35.

68. Coles, *Flannery O'Connor's South*, p. 36.

69. Coles, *Flannery O'Connor's South*, pp. 43–44.

70. C. Ross Mullins, "Flannery O'Connor: An Interview," *Jubilee* 11 (June 1963): 32–35. Rpt. in *Conversations with Flannery O'Connor*, ed. Magee, pp. 103–4.

71. Wood, "Flannery O'Connor's Racial Morals and Manners," p. 1078.

72. Wood, "Flannery O'Connor's Racial Morals and Manners," p. 1080.

Chapter 5

THE LAST DAYS

As the previous chapters illustrate, the 13 years that O'Connor spent living with her mother at Andalusia were filled with productivity: O'Connor wrote hundreds of letters, dozens of short stories and book reviews, and two novels; she entertained visitors; and she lectured around the country. Hovering in the background all this time, but perhaps in the foreground of her own mind, was the "red wolf" lupus. While it was always part of her life, she never drew attention to it and did everything she could to control it and bring some sense of normalcy to her life.

BIRDS, BIRDS, AND MORE BIRDS

Aside from her work and her associations with friends, O'Connor developed what appears to some to be a strange hobby: an intense interest in birds. O'Connor often referred wryly to an experience she had as a five year old, which she said was pivotal in her life: a photographer from New York came to her Savannah home to photograph a chicken she had that could walk forward and backward. As a child, she made clothing for her chickens, such as Colonel Eggbert who wore a white jacket which buttoned in the back and had a lace collar. She eventually developed an interest in many sorts of birds, including chickens, swans, ducks, geese, turkeys, and pheasants. Before they appeared much in her writing, birds appeared in her artwork. As previously mentioned, the cartoons she did for *The Colonnade* while at GSCW were signed with her initials "MFOC" in the shape of a bird, and in addition, a self-portrait she later painted includes a pheasant in the background.

But her passion was for peacocks. Her letters contain many references to them, including one particularly humorous one to Elizabeth Fenwick Way in which O'Connor mentions a peacock that snatched cigarettes from people and ate them. In her essay "King of the Birds," O'Connor admits that she has no real explanation for her fascination with these birds but that when she got her first one, which just happened to be around the time she was diagnosed with lupus, she could not stop looking at him in awe of his majesty. She often referred to the peacock as symbolic for Christ transfigured. Most often cited is her story "The Displaced Person," in which the priest says about a peacock displaying its tail, "Christ will come like that."[1] In "King of the Birds," she notes their stubborn, haughty attitude toward everything around them:

> When it suits him, the peacock will face you. Then you will see in a green-bronze arch around him a galaxy of gazing haloed suns. This is the moment when most people are silent.... I have never known a strutting peacock to budge a fraction of an inch for truck or tractor or automobile. It is up to the vehicle to get out of the way.[2]

While O'Connor claimed not to know the origin of her infatuation with birds, some believe that they were a distraction, and the tenacity of the peacock surely would have inspired her in her battle with lupus, the area from which she probably needed the most distraction but got the least. Throughout all the treatments and physical side effects she endured, she often concentrated on her spiritual growth. According to the way in which O'Connor perceived her circumstances, the real loss would not be in the productivity that she never fully reached because of the lupus but in a "refusal to accept unavoidable suffering and thus evolve further [spiritually]."[3] She was determined to carry out her vocation as a writer, but no one would have blamed her if she had become depressed after having to deal with her physical condition every day. "Under such circumstances, O'Connor could have sat on her mother's porch and rocked and fed her peafowl and waited to die."[4] Instead, she was writing constantly and eventually wrote what would be her last stories and letters from a hospital bed. She once admitted to fellow writer Miller Williams, "I don't have a lot of time. I can give a poem a couple of lines, a short story a paragraph, and a novel a few pages, then if I can stop reading without a sense of loss, I do, and I go on to something else."[5]

LUPUS REACTIVATED

It was in May 1964 that O'Connor became keenly aware that her lupus was active again, and it was to a hospital bed that she would soon be forced to retire. In November 1963, doctors detected an ovarian tumor, which needed to be surgically removed. She had considered hip replacement surgery earlier but had decided against it because surgery could reactivate her lupus. The surgery to remove the tumor carried the same risk but was unavoidable. With typical resignation and humor toward the inevitable, O'Connor had the surgery at Baldwin County Hospital in Milledgeville on February 25, and while it was successful, it did reactivate the lupus, as the doctors had feared. O'Connor was released from the hospital in March but underwent a course of antibiotics to treat a kidney infection and was eventually readmitted to the hospital due to the weakness and infections caused by the reactivated lupus.

In and out of the hospital during March and April of 1964, receiving blood transfusions, and taking medicines with horrid side effects, O'Connor seemed to know that her condition was serious. She was admitted to the Piedmont Hospital in Atlanta in May and developed dangerously high blood pressure. O'Connor insisted that she continue to write, even though she had to hide her work under her pillow lest she be chided by her mother and her doctors. She was released and returned to Milledgeville on June 20, but she was still not well. During this time, the tone of her letters changed little, but unlike letters written in the earlier stages of the disease, she did mention more often that she was very tired and had little energy. At the same time, she seemed to always keep in sight the spiritual benefits of her illness, namely the way in which it forced her to rely completely on God. She wrote to Betty Hester in a letter dated June 28, 1964, "Sickness before death is a very appropriate thing and I think those who don't have it miss one of God's mercies."[6]

THE END ARRIVES

Once O'Connor began to be in and out of the hospital, she wore down quickly and finally went into a coma on August 2. At 12:40 a.m. on August 3, 1964, Flannery O'Connor died of kidney failure at Baldwin County Hospital in Milledgeville. Her last letter had been written just six days earlier and was found by her mother near her bed. Appropriately, it is to her dear friend Maryat Lee. In the letter, she mentioned only that she had been too tired to type some stories she intended to send to Lee. As one might expect, the bulk of the letter expressed her concern for Lee, who had recently written to her about a threatening phone call she received, not for herself.

O'Connor's funeral was held on Tuesday, August 4, 1964, at Sacred Heart Catholic Church in Milledgeville; she was buried next to her father in Memory Hill Cemetery,[7] her grave marked with a flat, unassuming stone that reads the following:

MARY FLANNERY O'CONNOR
DAUGHTER OF REGINA LUCILLE CLINE
AND
EDWARD FRANCIS O'CONNOR, JR.
BORN IN SAVANNAH, GA
MARCH 25, 1925
DIED IN MILLEDGEVILLE, GA
AUGUST 3, 1964

In the years that followed, many wrote tributes to the life of one so talented that was cut so short. The reminiscences come from all eras of her life: from childhood friends, college friends, colleagues at Iowa and Yaddo, nuns, priests, and friends and writers from her adult years. Betty Boyd Love wrote, "Ours was an easy affection that never changed. It was hardly affected by either my increasing occupation with home and children or the increasing acclaim that was coming to Flannery. With me, she was always the delightful unliterary Flannery whom her friends treasured."[8] Perhaps one of the most apt statements concerning her life, her work, and her absence comes from Jean Loftus, who wrote, "Miss O'Connor is offering to men a vision of themselves as they really are. It is up to us now, regretting that she is no longer with us, to decide whether or not we shall share her vision."[9]

Over the years since her death, many of the things and people O'Connor held dearest have faded away. Perhaps because they always annoyed her or perhaps because they were a painful reminder of her daughter, Regina O'Connor gave O'Connor's peafowl away after her death: two were given to Our Lady of Perpetual Help cancer hospice in Atlanta, two were given to Stone Mountain Mansion at Stone Mountain National Park, and two were given to the Monastery of the Holy Ghost in Conyers, Georgia. The birds at Our Lady of Perpetual Help were sent to the Monastery of the Holy Ghost soon after their arrival because several of the patients complained about their screeching; the birds at Stone Mountain were soon eaten by other animals from the surrounding woods; and the birds at the monastery stayed until 1983 when a new abbot ordered the monk who took care of the peacocks to find them new homes. The peacocks went to live in Ohio, and their descendants survived until 1991 when a fox ate the last of them.

Many of the people dearest to her have since passed on as well. After moving back to the Cline-O'Connor house on Greene Street in Milledgeville and enduring several years of declining health, Regina O'Connor died in 1995 at age 99, three years older than O'Connor's goal of 96.[10] On the evening of December 26, 1998, O'Connor's close friend Betty Hester, who had struggled with depression most of her life, shot herself in the head at age 75, the same day she had given all of her unpublished manuscripts to William Sessions as he and his wife visited with her.[11] In June 2000, Sally Fitzgerald died at age 83.

A LEGACY

Even as those closest to O'Connor have diminished in number, her acclaim has grown. Her story collection *Everything that Rises Must Converge* was published posthumously in 1965; *The Complete Stories* was published in 1971 and was awarded the National Book Award by a unanimous vote after judges waived a rule saying the award could not be given to books by authors who had been dead more than two years. *The Flannery O'Connor Bulletin* was established in 1972 by Georgia College professors Rosa Lee Walston and Mary Barbara Tate, in 1992 Sura Rath established the Flannery O'Connor Society, and several conferences devoted to the discussion of her work are held annually. One of the most notable events occurred when the Milledgeville City Council declared 2003 "The Year of Reading Flannery O'Connor," distributed 250 copies of *The Complete Stories*, and sponsored several lectures and discussion groups. The Georgia College department of English, Speech, and Journalism also sponsors a periodic interdisciplinary Flannery O'Connor symposium. The most recent one was held in October 2003 and was entitled "Revelations: Flannery O'Connor, the Visionary and the Vernacular." This interdisciplinary celebration of O'Connor's life and work included writers such as Mary Gordon and Larry Brown, scholars Ralph Wood and Ben Alexander, artist Barry Moser, and several musical groups.

Several sites related to O'Connor's life have also been opened to the public since her death. On January 16, 1972, her mother donated her papers, manuscripts, and assorted personal items to Georgia College, prompting the creation of the Flannery O'Connor Memorial Room, where items such as her desk and books are on display, and the Flannery O'Connor Collection, which houses her papers and manuscripts. In addition, then Georgia Governor and later U.S. President Jimmy Carter declared the occasion Flannery O'Connor Day for the state. A marker was placed at her childhood home at 207 E. Charlton Street in Savannah in 1975, and O'Connor was the featured Georgian in Savannah in 1990 when the Flannery O'Connor Home Foundation was established and purchased the home in order to preserve it.

In addition, Andalusia was placed on the National Register of Historic Places in 1980, and the Flannery O'Connor-Andalusia Foundation was established in 1995. After Regina O'Connor moved into Milledgeville, Andalusia sat vacant and fell into disrepair. However, because of the Foundation's efforts, the main house is being restored. Visitors to the home can enter the main house and view the bedroom where O'Connor wrote, as well as several outbuildings and the surrounding landscape that surely provided the locale for most of her stories and the setting for much of her own life. According to Padgett Powell, "From a room in this house ... she saw Hulga (née Joy) Freeman, Ph.D., unwittingly give her wooden leg to a Bible salesman in a loft in a barn. She saw Mrs. May gored by her own handyman's bull ... She saw things that *thrill* people."[12] In September 2002, the Foundation opened the 21-acre farm complex for trolley tours; in March 2003, the main house and the grounds were opened for limited tours; and in October 2003, most of the first floor was opened for tours.

Without a doubt, O'Connor's place as a principal writer of the twentieth century was secure only a few years after her death. As Foder indicates, O'Connor's stories consistently appeared in literary anthologies by the early 1970s. In addition, O'Connor was the only contemporary female writer to appear on a 1982 survey of 50 college introductory American literature courses, and the Library of America published O'Connor's *Collected Works* in 1988, making her the only contemporary female writer and one of only five twentieth-century authors to be included.

O'Connor's influence has even extended beyond the academic world to include writers, musicians, and actors. For example, rock legend Bruce Springsteen, who began reading O'Connor's work when he was in his late 20s, credits her with portraying in her stories "a certain part of the American character that I was interested in writing about," leading him to delve into the type of characters he wanted to create in his musical narratives.[13] Late night talk show host Conan O'Brien and actor Tommy Lee Jones both wrote their theses at Harvard on O'Connor's work, and musical group U2 thanked O'Connor at the 1988 Grammy Awards. She has also been credited with influencing writers Louise Erdrich, Alice Walker, and Larry Brown; musician Jimmy Buffet; and actor Billy Bob Thornton.

While death can make nearly anyone into a saint, Flannery O'Connor was not perfect by any means. At times, she seemed callous, critical, and pessimistic. Yet, there can be no doubt that she also embodied the best of human qualities: devotion, sincerity, intellect, and independence. Like most of us, she knew many people over the course of her life, longed for deep relationships with others, and managed to achieve a few. At times geographically isolated by her lupus, she kept in contact with others mainly through her letters, the window into her most personal thoughts and a precious resource for those wishing to know Flannery O'Connor, the woman and the writer.

Interestingly enough, if we look at a list of the most prominent writers of her time, we see a list of names that many will recognize now: William Faulkner, Ernest Hemingway, Eudora Welty, Carson McCullers, Robert Penn Warren, Tennessee Williams, and so on. Surrounded by so many of great distinction, it would be easy for a single writer to fall through the cracks, especially one who lived for such a short time and produced relatively little. However, O'Connor's influence, popularity, and impact on American letters are secure. She was willing to do whatever it took to get the attention of a fallen world, and her often outlandish and startling characters and situations still shock, move, and stimulate her readers. While O'Connor might balk at any insinuation that she speaks to her readers from beyond the grave, there is no doubt that when we read of Mrs. Turpin or Joy/Hulga Hopewell or Hazel Motes or Tom T. Shiftlet, we hear from her. As Walter Clemons stated so well, "What we lost when she died is bitter. What we have is astonishing: the stories burn brighter than ever and strike deeper."[14]

NOTES

1. Flannery O'Connor, "The Displaced Person," *Collected Works*, ed. Sally Fitzgerald (New York: Library of America, 1988), p. 317.

2. O'Connor, "The King of the Birds," *Collected Works*, pp. 835–36.

3. Kathleen Spaltro, "When We Dead Awaken: Flannery O'Connor's Debt to Lupus," *The Flannery O'Connor Bulletin* 20 (1991): 36.

4. Lee Sturma, "Flannery O'Connor, Simone Weil, and the Virtue of Necessity," *Studies in Literary Imagination* 20, no. 3 (1987): 120.

5. Miller Williams, "Remembering Flannery O'Connor," in *Flannery O'Connor: In Celebration of Genius*, ed. Sarah Gordon (Athens, GA: Hill Street Press, 2000), p. 4.

6. Letter to "A," June 28, 1956, *The Habit of Being* (New York: Farrar, Straus, and Giroux, 1979), p. 163.

7. Jean W. Cash, *Flannery O'Connor: A Life* (Knoxville: University of Tennessee Press, 2002), p. 316–318.

8. Betty Boyd Love, "Recollections of Flannery O'Connor," *The Flannery O'Connor Bulletin* 14 (1985): 64.

9. Jean Loftus, "Flannery O'Connor: Linking Time and Eternity," unpublished essay, Flannery O'Connor Collection, Georgia College and State University, Milledgeville.

10. "Regina O'Connor, mother of author, dies here at age 99," *Union-Recorder* (Milledgeville, GA), May 9, 1995.

11. William Sessions, "Betty Hester: 'A Noble Soul,'" *Cheers!* (Fall/Winter 1998–99), http://library.gcsu.edu/~sc/hester.html.

12. Padgett Powell, "Andalusia is Open," *Oxford American* (July/August 2003): 30.

13. "Rock and Read: Will Percy Interviews Bruce Springsteen." *Double Take* 12 (Spring 1998). http://www.doubletakemagazine.org/mag/html/backissues/12/steen/index.html.

14. Julie F. Coryn, "Flannery O'Connor Day in Georgia," Press Release, Farrar, Straus, and Giroux, January 19, 1972.

SELECTED BIBLIOGRAPHY

WORKS ABOUT FLANNERY O'CONNOR

Books

Bain, Robert, and Joseph M. Flora. *Fifty Southern Writers After 1900: A Bio-Bibliographical Sourcebook*. New York: Greenwood Press, 1987.

Baker, Houston A., Martha Banta, Nina Baym, Scayan Bercovitch, Emory Elliott, Terence Martin, David Minter, Marjorie Perloff, and Daniel B. Shea. *Columbia Literary History of the United States*. New York: Columbia University Press, 1988.

Bloom, Harold, ed. *Modern Critical Views: Flannery O'Connor*. New York: Chelsea House Publishers, 1986.

———.*Twentieth-Century American Literature*. New York: Chelsea House Publishers, 1987.

Brantley, Will. *Feminine Sense in Southern Memoir: Smith, Glasgow, Welty, Hollman, Porter, and Hurston*. Jackson: University Press of Mississippi, 1993.

Cash, Jean W. *Flannery O'Connor: A Life*. Knoxville: University of Tennessee Press, 2002.

Davidson, Cathy N., Emory Elliott, Patrick O'Donnell, Valerie Smith, and Christopher P. Wilson. *The Columbia History of the American Novel*. New York: Columbia University Press, 1991.

Getz, Lorine M. *Flannery O'Connor: Her Life, Library and Book Reviews*. New York: Edwin Mellon Press, 1980.

Giannone, Richard. *Flannery O'Connor and the Mystery of Love*. Urbana, IL: University of Chicago Press, 1989.

————. *Flannery O'Connor: Hermit Novelist*. Urbana, IL: University of Chicago Press, 2000.

Gordon, Sarah, ed. *Flannery O'Connor: In Celebration of Genius*. Athens, GA: Hill Street Press, 2000.

Hoffman, Frederick, ed. *The Art of Southern Fiction: A Study of Some Modern Novelists*. Carbondale: Southern Illinois University Press, 1967.

Ketchin, Susan. *The Christ-Haunted Landscape: Faith and Doubt in Southern Fiction*. Jackson: University Press of Mississippi, 1994.

Kreying, Michael. *Inventing Southern Literature*. Jackson: University Press of Mississippi, 1998.

Magee, Rosemary M., ed. *Conversations with Flannery O'Connor*. Jackson: University Press of Mississippi, 1987.

Malin, Irving. *New American Gothic*. Carbondale: Southern Illinois University Press, 1962.

Meese, Elizabeth A. *Crossing the Double-Cross: The Practice of Feminist Criticism*. Chapel Hill: University of North Carolina Press, 1986.

Shinn, Thelma J. *Radiant Daughters: Fictional American Women*. New York: Greenwood Press, 1986.

Staton, Shirley F., ed. *Literary Theories in Praxis*. Philadelphia: University of Pennsylvania Press, 1987.

Periodicals

Babinec, Lisa S. "Cyclical Patterns of Domination and Manipulation in Flannery O'Connor's Mother-Daughter Relationships." *The Flannery O'Connor Bulletin* 19 (1990): 9–29.

Bandy, Stephen C. "'One of my babies': The Misfit and the Grandmother." *Studies in Short Fiction* 33, no. 1 (Winter 1996): 107–17.

Boren, Mark. "Flannery O'Connor, Laughter and the Word Made Flesh." *Studies in American Fiction* 26 (1998): 115–28.

Bottum, J. "Flannery O'Connor Banned." *Crisis* 18, no. 9 (October 2000): 48–49.

Butler, Rebecca R. "What's So Funny About Flannery O'Connor?" *The Flannery O'Connor Bulletin* 9 (1980): 30–40.

Carson, Anne Elizabeth. "'Break forth and wash the slime from this earth!': O'Connor's Apocalyptic Tornadoes." *Southern Quarterly* 40, no. 1 (Fall 2001): 19–27.

Coles, Robert. "Flannery O'Connor: Letters Larger than Life." *The Flannery O'Connor Bulletin* 8 (Autumn 1979): 6.

Emerson, Bo. "O'Connor Property a 'literary Graceland.'" *The Atlanta Journal-Constitution*, September 16, 2002.

Fitzgerald, Sally. "Root and Branch: O'Connor of Georgia." *Georgia Historical Quarterly* 64, no. 4 (1980): 377–87.

Gordon, Mary. "The Habit of Genius." Review of *The Habit of Being,* ed. by Sally Fitzgerald. *Saturday Review,* April 19, 1979, pp. 42–43.

Gordon, Sarah. "Flannery O'Connor and the Common Reader." *The Flannery O'Connor Bulletin* 10 (Autumn 1981): 38–45.

———. "Maryat and Julian and the 'not so bloodless revolution.'" *The Flannery O'Connor Bulletin* 21 (1992): 25–36.

Grau, Shirley Ann. "The O'Connor Letters: A Good Woman is Hard to Find." Review of *The Habit of Being,* ed. by Sally Fitzgerald. *Chicago Tribune,* March 25, 1979.

Gray, Paul. "Letters of Flannery O'Connor." Review of *The Habit of Being,* by Flannery O'Connor. *Time,* March 5, 1979, pp. 86–87.

Groover, Joel. "Author O'Connor's correspondent dies." *Atlanta Journal-Constitution,* December 30, 1998, p. B1.

Helmer, Shane. "Stumbling Onto the Spirit's Signposts." *Sojourners Magazine* 23, no. 10 (December 1994–January 1995): 18.

"Historical Marker Placed On O'Connor Birthplace." *Union-Recorder* (Milldegeville, GA), June 19, 1975.

Lee, Maryat. "Flannery, 1957." *The Flannery O'Connor Bulletin* 5 (Autumn 1976): 39–60.

Levering, Franz. "The Visionary Heart." *Atlanta Gazette,* February 19, 1975, p. 13.

Love, Betty Boyd. "Recollections of Flannery O'Connor." *The Flannery O'Connor Bulletin* 14 (1985): 64–71.

"Milledgeville reintroduced to native author." *Gwinnett Daily Post Online Edition* [Gwinnett County, Georgia]. 19 March 2003. http://www.gwinnettdaily-online.com/GDP/archive/articleED766996CC33404EADA14CB388B57 E10.asp.

"O'Connor Novel Good." Review of *The Violent Bear It Away,* by Flannery O'Connor. *Standard* (New Bedford, MA), n.d.

"O'Connor Peacocks Presented to Stone Mountain Plantation." *Union-Recorder* (Milledgeville, GA), January 13, 1972.

Osinski, Bill. "Fine-feathered epitaph: Final chapter comes for O'Connor's peacocks." *Union-Recorder* (Milledgeville, GA), December 6, 1991, pp. 1B–2B.

Paige, Linda Rohrer. "White Trash, Low Class, and No Class at All: Perverse Portraits of Phallic Power in Flannery O'Connor's *Wise Blood.*" *Papers on Language and Literature* 33, no. 3 (1997): 325–33.

Porter, Katherine Anne. "Gracious Greatness." *Esprit* 8, no. 1 (Winter 1964): 50–58.

Powell, Padgett. "Andalusia is Open." *Oxford American* (July/August 2003): 29–35.

Prenshaw, Peggy Whitman. "Divine Afflictions." Review of *Flannery O'Connor: A Life,* by Jean W. Cash. *Washington Post,* October 6, 2002, p. BW15.

Proffitt, Jennifer H. "Lupus and Corticosteroid Imagery in the Works of Flannery O'Connor." *The Flannery O'Connor Bulletin* 26–27 (1998–2000): 74–93.

Raymont, Henry. "Book Award to Flannery O'Connor." *The New York Times,* April 12, 1972, p. 34.

"Regina O'Connor, mother of author, dies here at age 99." *Union-Recorder* (Milledgeville, GA), May 9, 1995.

Sederberg, Nancy B. "Flannery O'Connor's Spiritual Landscape: A Dual Sense of Nothing." *The Flannery O'Connor Bulletin* 12 (Autumn 1983): 17–34.

Shannon, Margaret. "The World of Flannery O'Connor." *Atlanta Journal and Constitution Magazine,* February 20, 1972, pp. 8–9, 37–39.

Smith, Peter A. "Flannery O'Connor's Empowered Women." *American Scholar* 26, no. 2 (Spring 1994): 34–47.

Spaltro, Kathleen. "When We Dead Awaken: Flannery O'Connor's Debt to Lupus." *The Flannery O'Connor Bulletin* 20 (1991): 33–44.

Sturma, Lee. "Flannery O'Connor, Simone Weil, and the Virtue of Necessity." *Studies in Literary Imagination* 20, no. 3 (1987): 102–21.

Tate, J.O. "On Flannery O'Connor: Citizen of the South and Citizen of the World." *The Flannery O'Connor Bulletin* 13 (Autumn 1984): 26–43.

Trowbridge, Clinton W. "The Comic Sense of Flannery O'Connor: Literalist of the Imagination." *The Flannery O'Connor Bulletin* 12 (Autumn 1983): 77–92.

Weber, Ronald. "A Good Writer is Hard to Find." *Catholic Dossier* 5, no. 4 (July–August 1999): 30–32.

Wellborn, Amy. "Flannery O'Connor Banned in Opelousas." *Our Sunday Visitor,* September 10, 2000. http://amywelborn.com/flannery/banned.html.

———. "Flannery O'Connor: Stalking Pride." *Our Sunday Visitor* (August 8, 1999).

Wells, Joel. "A Genius Who Frustrated Critics." Review of *Flannery O'Connor: The Complete Stories,* by Flannery O'Connor. *National Catholic Reporter,* November 19, 1971.

White, Terry. "Allegorical evil, existentialist choice in O'Connor, Oates and Styron." *The Midwest Quarterly,* Vol. 34, 1993.

Whitt, Margaret. "Flannery O'Connor's Ladies." *The Flannery O'Connor Bulletin* 15 (1986): 42–50.

Wood, Ralph C. "Flannery O'Connor's Racial Morals and Manners." *The Christian Century* 111, no. 33 (16 Nov. 1994): 1076–81.

———. "Where Is the Voice Coming From? Flannery O'Connor on Race." *The Flannery O'Connor Bulletin* 22 (1993–1994): 90–118.

Wray, Virginia. "The Importance of Home to the Fiction of Flannery O'Connor." *Renascence* 47 (Winter 1995): 103–15.

Wylder, Jean. "Flannery O'Connor: A Reminiscence and Some Letters." *North American Review* (Spring 1970): 58–65.

Young, Robin Darling. "Flannery O'Connor: *The Collected Works.*" *First Things First* 101 (March 2000): 59–60.

Documents from the Flannery O'Connor Collection at Georgia State College and University

Coryn, Julie F. "Flannery O'Connor Day in Georgia." Press Release. Farrar, Straus, and Giroux, 19 Jan. 1972.

"Flannery O'Connor." *Talk of the Nation.* Hosted by Melinda Penkava. National Public Radio, May 22, 1997.

"Georgia Writer's Correspondence with Flannery O'Connor and Her Extensive Library, Discovered After Her Suicide." *Weekend All Things Considered.* Hosted by Jacki Lyden. National Public Radio, February 6, 1999.

Harold, DeVene. Unpublished essay. Flannery O'Connor Collection. Georgia College and State University, Milledgeville.

Kevin, Sister Mary. "Flannery O'Connor: The Vision of Man." Unpublished essay. Flannery O'Connor Collection. Georgia College and State University, Milledgeville.

Loftus, Jean. "Flannery O'Connor: Linking Time and Eternity." Unpublished essay. Flannery O'Connor Collection. Georgia College and State University, Milledgeville.

Nelson, Ed. "Religious Experience with Flannery O'Connor." Address. Georgia College, Milledgeville, April 20, 1975.

O'Connor, Flannery. Address. Georgia State College for Women, January 7, 1960.

Internet Sources

The Aesthetics of Incongruity: The Tortured Existence of Flannery O'Connor. http://www.geocities.com/flannery42_2000/index.html.

"Authors in Depth: Flannery O'Connor." *The Meyer Literature Site.* http://www.bedfordstmartins.com/literature/bedlit/authors_depth/oconnor.htm.

"Books and Writers: Flannery O'Connor." http://www.kirjasto.sci.fi/flannery.htm.

The Comforts of Home: A Repository of Flannery O'Connor Information. http://www.mediaspecialist.org/.

"Flannery O'Connor." *Fantastic Fiction.* http://www.fantasticfiction.co.uk/authors/Flannery_OConnor.htm.

"Flannery O'Connor." *Heroes of History.* http://www.heroesofhistory.com/page82.html.

"Flannery O'Connor: 1925–1964." *Georgia Women of Achievement.* http://www.gawomen.org/honorees/oconnorf.htm.

"Flannery O'Connor: 1925–1964." *Little Blue Light.* http://www.littlebluelight.com/lblphp/intro.php?ikey=20.

The Flannery O'Connor-Andalusia Foundation. http://www.andalusiafarm.org/.

"Flannery O'Connor Biography." http://www.geocities.com/flannery42_2000/biography.html.

The Flannery O'Connor Collection. http://library.gcsu.edu/~sc/foc.html.

Jensen, Susan. "Classic Authors: Flannery O'Connor." Pub. Aug. 24, 1999. http://www.suite101.com/article.cfm/classic_literature/24579.

"The Life of Flannery O'Connor." http://gographics.com/funnies/flann1.htm.

Lupus Foundation of America. http://www.lupus.org/.

"Mary Flannery O'Connor (1924–1964)." *Twentieth Century American Women Writers.* http://faculty.ccc.edu/wr-womenauthors/pinkver/oconnor.htm.

"Q&A about Flannery O'Connor." http://www.eiu.edu/~eng1002/authors/o'connor2/qanda.htm.

Reuben, Paul P. "Chapter 10: Late Twentieth Century: 1945 to the Present—Flannery O'Connor." *PAL: Perspectives in American Literature—A Research and Reference Guide.* http://www.csustan.edu/english/reuben/pal/chap10/oconnor.

"The SAC LitWeb Flannery O'Connor Page." http://www.accd.edu/sac/english/bailey/oconnorf.htm.

Sessions, William. "Passing by the Dragon." http://www.middleenglish.org/Pages/htrfo.htm.

A Student's Guide to Flannery O'Connor. http://www.geocities.com/Athens/Troy/2188/.

"Yaddo and Flannery O'Connor." http://library.gcsu.edu/~sc/focyaddo.html.

SELECTED WORKS BY FLANNERY O'CONNOR

Wise Blood. New York: Harcourt, 1952.

A Good Man Is Hard To Find. New York: Harcourt, 1955. Published in England as *The Artificial Nigger.* London: Neville Spearman, 1957.

The Violent Bear It Away. New York: Farrar, Straus, and Giroux, 1960.

A Memoir of Mary Ann (editor and author of introduction). New York: Farrar, Straus, and Giroux, 1962. Published in England as *Death of a Child.* London: Burns & Oates, 1961.

Three by Flannery O'Connor. New York: Signet, 1964.

Everything That Rises Must Converge. New York: Farrar, Straus, and Giroux, 1965.

Mystery and Manners: Occasional Prose. Ed. Sally and Robert Fitzgerald. New York: Farrar, Straus, and Giroux, 1969.

The Complete Short Stories. New York: Farrar, Straus, and Giroux, 1971.

The Habit of Being. Ed. Sally Fitzgerald. New York: Farrar, Straus, and Giroux, 1979.

The Presence of Grace and Other Book Reviews. Ed. Carter W. Martin. Athens, GA: University of Georgia Press, 1983.

Collected Works (contains *Wise Blood, A Good Man Is Hard To Find, The Violent Bear It Away, Everything That Rises Must Converge*, and selected letters, stories, and occasional prose). Ed. Sally Fitzgerald. New York: Library of America, 1988.

INDEX

About the Author

MELISSA SIMPSON is a writing instructor at Hendrix College. She has previously published articles on Toni Morrison, Pat Conroy, and Robert Frost.